Poppyganda

REMEMBER
FORGET

THE HISTORICAL & SOCIAL IMPACT OF A FLOWER

MATTHEW LEONARD

FOREWORD BY LT. COL. ALEX TURNER D.S.O.

UNIFORM
PRESS

Uniform Press Ltd
66 Charlotte Street
London W1T 4QE

© Matthew Leonard, 2015
www.uniformpress.co.uk

A catalogue record for this book is available
from the British Library

ISBN 978-1-910500-163

Cover design Uniform Press Ltd
Typeset by Vivian@Bookscribe

Printed and bound in Great Britain

Contents

8   Foreword

10   Introduction

24   The Battle-zones of Modern War

52   A History of the Remembrance Poppy

78   The Twenty-first Century Western Front

102   The Future of the Past

122   Epilogue

126   Reference/Bibliography

(Pages 6–7) The art installation 'Blood Swept Lands and Seas of Red' at the Tower of London. Created by artists Paul Cummins and Tom Piper, 888,246 ceramic poppies progressively filled the Tower's famous moat between 17 July and 11 November 2014. Each poppy represented a British military fatality during the First World War. (© Crown copyright 2014)

For Georgia Rose

Foreword

Throughout history soldiers have placed huge value in symbols. The Roman eagle, the Mongol totemic standard, the Crusader's Cross and the Ottoman *arma* are but a few examples. As British soldiers we are no exception. The colours – battle flags – that we carry revere the names of places we have fought. The insignia, medals and other badges of rank denote regimental identity, personal experience or qualifications.

And, for a few weeks every year, we wear a paper poppy. It is incorporated into our uniforms behind cap badges or buttons and, where that is not practical, pinned on.

As Matt Leonard makes so clear in this lucid and impressively objective study, the poppy means different things to different people – and has done over time. From its inception in the wake of the Great War to its continuing significance in contemporary Britain, it has tracked and even driven shifts in the part that collective 'remembrance' plays in our national life.

For me the poppy symbolises one thing – and one thing only. Sacrifice. Any period in uniform brings it in some measure. Relationships damaged by long absences; the sum of actions we may have been called upon to do that prey on one's mind for life. And, for some, the scars of physical injury.

The ultimate sacrifice is death and in this context the poppy represents all those comrades, known and unknown, who crossed that great divide. Sometimes blissfully quickly. Sometimes twisting in pain and fear as their friends battled to keep them among the living. As it is so often put, they gave 'everything'. Everything they ever had. Everything to come. Violent deaths are premature deaths.

That is the essence of the poppy for the British soldier: a mark of respect for people who put themselves – or found themselves – in harm's way, in the service of their country and fellow citizens.

For a decade now I have volunteered whenever possible to take donations for the annual Poppy Appeal on the King's Road in London. Increasingly I find that foreigners approach me to ask what I am collecting for. Once I have explained, without a single exception, these French, Americans, Russians, Germans, Japanese and others gladly make a donation even if some chose not to take a flower. It is heartening to see, irrespective of historical and cultural barriers, that such is the universal respect for sacrifice invested in this simple symbol of nature.

Like all symbols, the poppy can be manipulated and reinvented. This is of primarily academic interest, as Matt Leonard demonstrates here. It is a necessary conversation and I applaud him for contributing to it. But I will continue to wear one every year – and collect, when I can, for the appeal – because of what that little paper flower means to me personally.

I choose to see it as a fragment from the world of conflict and sacrifice I have travelled through; a very different world to the one we inhabit in our everyday lives and one where countless forebears, including some of my friends and comrades, lived their last moments.

Lieutenant Colonel Alexander Turner DSO, Irish Guards

Introduction

Warfare has always been a bloody business. In every conflict ever fought the basic premise has been to kill as many of the enemy as possible, or at least more of him than he of you.

The staggering casualty figures of the First World War (and indeed the Second) were not the result of a heightened animosity or willingness to kill absent from history's previous

Over the top, and into the strange new world of twentieth-century war. (*Publisher's Collection*)

conflicts. It was that by 1914 the ability to destroy the enemy had advanced exponentially since the last great European conflagration. The technological and industrial revolutions that swept through Europe after Waterloo had altered the concept of warfare from a series of single day battles on a clearly defined field of play into an industrial undertaking, committed over a vast area of time and space. Armies now numbered in their millions, and soldiers could be efficiently mobilised and quickly transported over great distances using

Europe's impressive railway networks. The weaponry these modern armies had at their disposal was unimaginably destructive, and able to be deployed at a greater range and fired faster and for longer than ever before. More importantly, those on the front lines could now be continually resupplied with everything from food and water to ammunition and matériel. The logistics of killing had been refined. By the war's end, firing over a million shells in a single day was easily achievable. On 21st March 1918, the opening of the great *Kaiserschlacht* offensive, the Germans fired over three thousand shells a minute at the British lines in the space of five hours. Such a display of force had never been witnessed before, and even today it is hard to appreciate the destruction a bombardment of that magnitude would cause.

This terrifying power forms the basis of Britain's macabre fascination with the conflict. Even though the Second World War was far bloodier (the Russians alone lost around 27 million dead between 1941 and 1945) it claimed approximately half the number of British lives. The Great War's fighting was more localised and intensely violent than any previous conflict Britain had been involved in. It was also increasingly accessible to the public via photography, film and a modernising media. The impact was so great that by 1940 this sort of warfare was no longer a new phenomenon – the idea of total war

POPPYGANDA

was ingrained in the public conscious and people were well aware of the damage that advanced weaponry could inflict on human flesh. The shock factor had dissipated. After all, the hundreds of thousands of wounded soldiers that the First World War left bleeding in its wake had been back in public life for more than two decades, a legion of living reminders to the horrors of industrial war.

Although there was outrage at the 500 or so deaths caused by the German bombing of Coventry in 1940, that some 450 planes had reached the English city that night was not particularly surprising. This was how war was now waged – a grotesque numbers game where the victor

The shattered remains of Coventry Cathedral. By 1940 battlefields had become battle-zones. (*Wiki*)

Winston Churchill visiting the ruins of Coventry Cathedral. (*Wiki*)

would be the side that projected the greatest industrial might. By 1943, when the Allies bombed Hamburg, flying thousand-plane missions was nothing out of the ordinary and the thirty thousand people mostly burned to death on 28th July seemed somehow acceptable. It was the cost of war. Compare this to the British casualty figures on the 1st July 1916, a day that will forever be known as the 'bloodiest day of the British Army'. Half as many again were killed during a single night in Hamburg, the majority of whom were civilians, yet it is rarely mentioned in the same breath as that fateful summer's day in Picardy. (That the French Army lost almost 28,000 dead in a single August day in 1914 is also not widely known in Britain.)

Once the idea of total war took hold, it changed the notion of conflict forever. Bombing raids on cities were more common than might be imagined during the First World War. Civilians were caught up in the fighting and as men went off to the front, women became intrinsic to the machinations of modern conflict, children lied about their ages to sign up and older members of society took up arms to defend Britain's shores from invasion. For the first time

Hamburg after a series of bombing raids.

Women workers with shells in Chilwell filling factory, 1917.
(IWM Q30040)

warfare was all consuming, and as the violence meted out on the battlefields escalated, nature was destroyed at the same rate as people, forging new links between mankind and the landscapes of war.

The iconic pictures of the Western Front show a world without form, the literal representation of Blunden's notion that 'mud, death and life were the same thing'.[1] Never before had warfare destroyed the landscape on which it was fought to such a violent extent. Swathes of northern Europe were dug up to create deep and complex defensive systems. The Western Front, regardless of its geology, became riddled with tunnels, dug outs and deep shelters. Natural caves were expanded and huge man-made voids were created, consuming soldiers from within and turning battlefields into battle-zones. Idyllic countryside and rural communities were transformed into quagmires of blood, filth and misery. Villages and towns were shelled into oblivion, ground to dust. Soldiers were not just shot or wounded from musket or cannon-fire. Now they were often immolated, atomised by shells that were larger than the men that fired them. Many died without a trace, their bodies disappearing into the earth, becoming one with it, only to be blown up and reinterred again, and again, and again. To survive in this chaos, in this completely alien world of darkness, death and destruction, often with no horizon or point of reference, soldiers utilised their base instincts and senses, slithering closer to their primeval roots. The manner in which the human senses interacted with the new environment of war changed dramatically. Men lived in the earth and not on it, entwining them with nature, as humanity, wildlife, land and society were all ground down into a homogenous grave.

In the midst of this cauldron, a place where little, if anything, would grow, and most things would quickly die, one flower steadily became more and more prevalent. The way it would bloom on the parapet of trenches, or out in No Man's Land, in the maelstrom of searing iron, meant that it quickly came to symbolise the new found connections between people and objects; humans, matériel and landscape were as much being sown into the once verdant fields of France and Belgium as they were into the complex fabric of twentieth-century society. As the war continued, the human cost accelerated far beyond its accepted price and off into the realm of nightmares. It is said that every family in Britain lost somebody in the war, and while this may be an exaggeration, losses were nevertheless deeply felt by many communities, particularly those where the Pal's Battalions were recruited. The result was grieving on a national scale.

Such epic losses could not be dealt with as they had been before. These were more public, brought home to the people of Britain in the daily casualty lists printed in the press, or in the presence of absence felt in the streets. Casualties were so numerous that early on it was decided the bodies of the fallen would not be repatriated, denying bereaved families the emotional closure of a funeral, or a local grave by which to mourn. It was not long before these issues reached the forefront of public, political and military life, something that persuaded Fabien Ware to try and ensure the resting places of all who had died were recorded for posterity. In 1915, Ware's efforts were officially recognised by the inauguration of the Graves Registration Commission (later to be known as the Imperial War Graves Commission and finally, as we know it today, the Commonwealth War Graves Commission).

It was not until the war's end that the Commission's work could really begin. The first task was to secure the land necessary to bury so many. By the end of 1918, the Commission had identified more than 587,000 graves, and recognised that almost as many of the dead, some 559,000, had none. It was the Commission's task to create a soothing blanket of memory and remembrance, something to ameliorate the brutal realties of the savaged battle-zones, both at home and abroad. The greatest architects of the day were instructed to create the plethora of monuments, cemeteries and memorials that now cover northern France, Belgium and elsewhere. They were like nothing seen before. In this new and confusing landscape of memory and loss, the remembrance poppy could take root and quickly blossom in the imagination of a grieving public, standing alongside the shining Portland stone memorials

CWGC Headstone carving. *(Wiki)*

as a more personal object, one able to reflect the outpouring of public grief and despair on an individual level.

The poppy has always been an enduring symbol and is the subject of many books, television programmes and no little controversy. The links between the different genus of poppy, remembrance and pain, war and peace, politics and money are often ambiguous and always complex. Professor Nicholas J Saunders' book on the subject[2] tells how these connections can be traced back to the time of the Trojan Wars, and even before, and how they still exist in today's conflict in Afghanistan. As an object, the flower, its history and multiple meanings are worthy of a PhD thesis in their own right. However, it is not the intention here to discuss this artefact's oeuvre, rather to demonstrate how the destruction caused by the First World War forged new links between man, nature, landscape and objects. War was now fought in the earth, the dead occupied the same space as the living and as the many 'missing' were integrated into the fabric of the battle-zones, the human emotions of guilt, loss, memory, fear, hatred and love became encased in the red paper petals of the remembrance poppy.

This book will explore these links, starting with the character of the First World War's battle-zones, exploring how they differed from the previous battlefields of war, demonstrating how and why modern warfare simultaneously creates as it destroys. It will then discuss how the poppy became the symbol of the tragic losses necessitated by industrialised war, and over time metastasised into a political weapon in its own right. It is a story of altruism, greed, nationalism, technology, media power, selfless sacrifice and public and private agenda. Not all the belligerent nations embraced the poppy, and those that did were not always unified in their approaches. If the poppy seemingly symbolises so much to the British, what does it mean to the Commonwealth countries or former British colonies that are now independent? How do the

The war destroyed everything in its path, people, nature and society were ground to dust all along the front. (*Library of Congress*)

French, the Germans, the Belgians, the Americans and so many other nations regard this famous flora?

Today's Western Front will also be explored, highlighting how the poppy and its fellow objects of memory have laid down an intangible, but nevertheless embracing, new layer to the old battlefields, changing them forever and diluting their true history. In a world where the massed pitch battles of the early twentieth century no longer have a place in warfare, what will the future hold for the remembrance poppy? Once 11th November 2018 has passed, will this symbol fade, just as the sound of the guns did a hundred years before? Or are the emotional connections to this flower, and the deep-seated human feelings it has the power to evoke, too ingrained in our conscious to ever be forgotten? Most importantly, has the poppy now become a symbol of propaganda, something so removed from its original purpose that it offers a dangerous commentary on modern warfare, politics and the barbarity of man?

Notes

1. Blunden, E. (2009). Undertones of War. London: Penguin Classics. P 98.
2. Saunders, N. J. (2013). The Poppy: A Cultural History from Ancient Egypt to Flanders Fields and Afghanistan. London: Oneworld.

The Battle-zones of Modern War

Soon after August 1914, most preconceived ideas of what form a modern battlefield should take were banished forever, long before the demise of that bleakest of years. No matter how bloody or violent warfare had previously become, pejoratively speaking, battles had been waged over a relatively short period and on a localised piece of ground. Said terrain was inevitably affected by events, but only to a certain extent. Armies could be, and frequently were, huge, the new military technologies of the day would always be employed, and efforts dedicated to killing the enemy were pursued with vigour. Yet battles almost always ended relatively quickly because armies were worn out through the sheer exhaustion of giving battle. The mind was willing, but the body was weak.

Industrial war changed all this. At the Battle of Neuve Chapelle in 1915, the ferocity of modern conflict destroyed the few still lingering notions that this war would be like those that had preceded it. The British unleashed more shells on the German positions in just half an hour than they had fired during the entire Boer War. In this conflict soldiers on the front lines were being mercilessly pounded for weeks by long-range artillery, and these heavy weapons were fed with a seemingly endless supply of shells – a much easier task for the human body than forming square, or standing in a thin red line. The machine gun could do the job of a hundred riflemen, and new chemical weapons had the ability to bring entire battalions to their knees with little effort required on the part of the attacker. Of course, the path to mutual destruction didn't always run smoothly, and all sides suffered shortages as their economies geared up to wage total war. Before Neuve Chapelle, shell production in Britain was so lacklustre that many guns were reputedly reduced to firing only a handful of shot a day. Germany struggled to produce adequate quantities of cordite, and France was forced to face up to the loss of so much of her raw material producing territory.

Yet these were mere teething problems. By 1917, Britain and her Empire were producing more than fifty million shells a year, and by the war's end the British Army had unleashed over 170 million shells on its enemies. France underwent a similar transformation of fortunes, increasing her daily production of 75mm shells for her extremely effective field gun from less than 4,000 per month at the end of 1914 to over 150,000 a month by the start of the Somme battles some 18 months later. Even Germany quadrupled her production of shells during the first two years of the war, achieving a figure of almost 40 million a year by 1916. Germany's rail links to the Fatherland, France's internal transport systems and Britain's Royal Navy ensured that all sides eventually forged out efficient supply chains, and with the production of armaments continuing apace, by 1916, battles on the scale of Verdun and the Somme became a reality. Halfway through the war, the mind was still willing, and the body was no longer weak.

Without the political will to industrialise warfare it is doubtful whether the iconic and tragic clashes of 1916 and later could have been fought, at least on the same scale. But all sides knew that once the lines had bogged down, there would have to be a period of attritional annihilation – Douglas Haig had predicted it long before 1914 – and to win this grisly contest, numbers would be vital. Trench warfare rapidly descended into a gruesome slogging match. The only way to victory was to grind one's opponent to dust. If they kill a million of us, and we kill a million and one of them, we win. That was how the commanders of the day saw the situation, and given the contemporary understanding of technology, communications and strategy, there were few, if any, other options available to them. Yet the use of advanced weaponry, on such a massive scale, to kill unprecedented numbers of the enemy, had a by-product that was not fully appreciated by those in charge – high explosives and a mechanised approach to warfare did not just annihilate people, but also the landscape on which they fought.

In many of the war's theatres, and particularly on the

Western Front, the only refuge from the hot metallic air was the ground itself. Never in the history of warfare had soldiers lived in such proximity to the earth. The trenches of the Western Front were not a new concept, but the scale they were created on certainly was. While at the front, many would never see anything but the sky above them and the chalk or mud of their trench walls. Vision became severely restricted as a result and the crenulation of trenches only made things worse. Accordingly, the way that the senses operated began to change. In the chaos of a front line position, reliance on sight became a luxury that few could afford. After all, weaponry could be felt for far quicker than it could be seen, gas could be smelled without having to raise a nose above the parapet, and the differing sounds that shells made as they approached revealed their type and where they would land. Together, these changes required twentieth century soldiers to forget the ways of modern civilian life and regress back to an earlier time. Embracing the previously lost sensorial perspective of the animal to keep them alive.

What could be seen from the surface of the Western Front, like the proverbial iceberg, was only part of the whole. The trench lines were but the ramparts of a submerged fortress. Beneath them, hidden from view, were the real fortifications. Deep down, fighting tunnels, listening posts and mine chambers took the fight directly to the enemy, while laterals protected the lines. Often, the deep subterranean side of trench warfare is portrayed as a secret war – a hidden battlefield where devious tactics were employed to destroy the enemy from within. Yet in many ways this perspective dilutes the truth. Digging forward towards the enemy with the intention of blowing up his defences was clearly something that had to be done with the utmost secrecy. Each side had many listening tunnels and stations in No Man's Land constantly searching for the approach of enemy sappers. Yet to reduce subterranean warfare to a 'weapon' is to fundamentally misunderstand the nature of the Western Front's battle-zones and the human experience of 'being in' them.

The vast crater at La Boisselle on the Somme, standing alone, a huge scar in the fabric of the Western Front, demonstrates the power of mine warfare, yet it was one of 23 mines blown by the British along the Somme battlefront on the 1st July 1916 (although some were far bigger than others, and not all were designed to destroy the enemy's positions). The crater from the Hawthorn Ridge mine not far away is actually bigger than the one at Lochnagar, as a second mine was detonated in the same place a few months later. This double crater near blood-soaked Beaumont Hamel is perhaps not as well known, and certainly not as well visited, even though the explosion that caused it was immortalised in Malins' 1916 film. Today the Hawthorn crater is covered in trees and dense foliage, yet the first mine

La Boisselle mine crater
The largest mine crater on the Western Front was created when the British blew two huge ammonal charges (36,000 lbs and 24,000 lbs) under a German position known as 'Schwaben Hohe'. The crater originally measured approximately 91 m across and 25 m deep. The blast obliterated around 120 m of German trenches and collapsed at least nine dug outs. (*IWM Q1480*)

detonation there was the biggest man-made explosion in history, at least for the eight minutes that passed until the La Boisselle mines were blown. The act of digging the tunnels and laying the mines for these subterranean explosions was clearly secret, but the knowledge that there were so many mines blown that day highlights how this side of the fighting was not ephemeral, but rather intrinsic to waging trench warfare. All sides adopted this offensive (and sometimes defensive) posture and the Somme is by no means unique with its deep subterranean elements.

Between 1915 and 1918, 519 mines were detonated at the Butte de Vauquois near Verdun, in an area of front measuring just 460m wide by 340m deep. On the Izonzo front, mines were laid inside mountains and glaciers, and across the Western Front mine warfare was an almost daily occurrence. At Hill 60 and along the rest of the Messines Ridge, on the heights of Vimy and in the depths of the surrounding Labyrinth, across the Chemin des Dames, amongst the forests of the Argonne and inside the subterranean forts of Verdun, right down to Le Ligne in the mountains of the Vosges (where the defensive systems were carved out of rock and granite), subterranean war was vital to both attack and defence. This was not a secret war. It was as much a part of trench warfare as the trenches themselves. Just as the poppy's roots grew from below the surface, so did the concept of trench warfare, steadily blending man, the earth, nature and war together, creating the literal and figurative foundations of the Western Front.

Despite the number of offensive tunnels constructed, the destruction of the enemy from below was arguably the smaller part of the war underground. The proliferation of more extensive long-range weapons afforded the defender the ability to lay down huge volumes of fire on the attacker's reserve lines, choking off reinforcements before they could reach the fighting. The casualty figures for the 1st July 1916 reflect this, with many soldiers blown to pieces before they even reached a front line trench. Co-ordination between the different parts of the Army was not as it should have been that day. Russian Saps (shallow tunnels) had been dug out into No Man's Land for men to attack along, allowing soldiers to appear in front of the German lines in relative safely, or be adapted for use as forward mortar and machine gun positions, but they were not employed. One tunnelling officer recalled looking back at the British lines from the relative safety of a sap exit in No Man's Land, watching hundreds of men being cut down. It was a tragic error in communication and understanding, but one that was not to be repeated.

Many of the German units along the Somme front had been in situ since 1914 and 1915, giving them plenty of time to construct complex underground systems beneath their trenches. The German stormtrooper, Ernst Jünger, told of how when building these places wood and concrete were regularly used.[1] Electricity and even hot and cold running water were also common features. The shelters were deep enough to withstand the heaviest bombardment, and contributed to the hideous outcome of that summer's day. The underground workings at Beaumont Hamel allegedly took the form of a subterranean village, sheltering men in relative comfort deep in the bowels of the earth.[2]

By the middle of 1916, the subterranean effort had reached its peak. Along with the trenches came dugouts, deep dugouts and now entire underground systems comprising of subways (communication tunnels for the transport of men and equipment), existing souterraines (underground quarries), hospitals, dormitories, head-quarters, kitchens, latrines, chapels and even cemeteries. On the eve of the Battle of Arras in April 1917, less than a year after the Battle of the Somme, over 24,000 men waited in the expanded cave system beneath the town, ready to funnel up into the front line trenches. At the same time, on Vimy Ridge, the Canadian and British forces waited in safety in over a dozen subways, ready to charge the German positions on the summit of Hill 145. Along the Chemin des Dames, there were over 370 known souterraines, many of which were used by the Germans and the French to shield their men. Famously, at the *Drachenhöhle* (Dragon Cavern), which lay beneath a pinch point on the Chemin des Dames, the Germans and French shared the same souterraine, building internal walls by mutual consent, continuing the war underground as if on the surface. At Vauquois on the edge of the Argonne and only 25 kilometres from Verdun, beneath the eponymously named Butte, lay over seventeen kilometres of tunnels, some more than a hundred metres deep. The message was clear. The further men could go underground, on as greater scale as possible, the safer they would be.

Within the space of two years, hundreds of thousands of soldiers had managed to adapt to a totally alien world, one of mud, clay, earth, chalk and darkness, where life was felt, tasted, heard and smelled, yet seldom seen. This brought them closer to nature, to fauna and flora, forming new connections with the earth, and new relationships between the soldier and his environment. In effect, a new culture, defined by the landscape it had created, and the methods it used to engage with it, was born. As the violent abuse being meted out above led to the creation of a new world below, it also produced a unique landscape on the surface. A great strip of the French and Belgian countryside was being pulverised, torn to shreds, obliterated on a hitherto unknown scale, and reshaped into a new world, the boundaries of which dissolved into the often grey and putrid horizon. In much the same way human bodies were being destroyed. Powerful weaponry did not distinguish between man and landscape. It claimed victims of all that stood in its path.

This contortion of nature did not go unnoticed by those in the firing line. As the land was destroyed and reborn it changed into something far more sinister. To many it seemed alive; taking revenge on those that would wish it harm. The ubiquitous mud seemed to suck men to their doom, becoming a sentient killing machine that could compete with Krupp or Vickers. Santanu Das, in his excellent book, *Touch and Intimacy in First World War Literature*[3], describes how this changing relationship between man and nature was reflected in the language used by those who wrote of their war experiences. The front was described using anthropomorphic terminology. The earth was regarded as 'gaunt and skeletal', the men that occupied it 'burrowed and slithered' through the mud, and the destruction of landscape was often termed 'murderous'. The filth and mud was said to creep and crawl, actually seeking out men to destroy. Jack Dillon, a Lewis Gunner at Passchendaele described how:

> *The mud there wasn't liquid, it wasn't porridge, it was a curious kind of sucking kind of mud. When you got off track with your load, it 'drew' at you, not like quicksand, but a real monster that sucked at you.*[4]

These descriptions are found time and time again in contemporary poetry and prose. A front line newspaper from 1917 carried an article depicting the landscape as a hideous monster:

> *At night, crouching in a shell-hole and filling it, the mud watches, like an enormous octopus. The victim arrives. It throws its poisonous slobber out at him, blinds him, closes around him, buries him… For men die of mud, as they die from bullets, but more horribly.*[5]

It is this last line that really encapsulates the feeling of many soldiers. The landscape could kill a man far 'more horribly' than the modern weapons of war. This understanding of the land, a connection and empathy with it, cemented the new relationship with the battle-zone into the mind of the soldier, some of whom could in turn pass on this concept to the public at home.

J R R Tolkien was not on the Western Front for long, but he did experience life in the trenches of the Somme, and what he referred to as 'the animal horror' never left him.[6] Tolkien was a Second Lieutenant in the 11th Lancashire Fusiliers in July 1916. He missed the infamous opening day of the battle as his battalion was held in reserve, but two weeks later he was hurled into the maelstrom. Tolkien spent the next four months or so at the front, taking part in several major attacks, most notably the disastrous charge on Ovillers. In the end it was not shellfire or bullets that brought him down but trench fever, from which he never really recovered. Nevertheless, his experience influenced his portrayal of the bleak, muddy and barren landscape in *The Lord of the Rings*. In 1960, he wrote 'The Dead Marshes and the approaches to the Morannon owe something to Northern France after the Battle of the Somme.'[7] In *The Lord of The Rings* Sam Gamgee refers to seeing 'dead things, dead faces in the water,'[8] beneath the stinking muddy mire of the Dead Marshes, very likely a reference to corpses witnessed by Tolkien in the mud of the Somme.

Much of the contemporary art mirrors Tolkien's thoughts. Otto Dix's *Flanders,* or Nash's *We are Making a New World* show how people were becoming one with the landscape, in some works, particularly *Flanders,* each is barely distinguishable from the other. The Germans have always had a relationship with nature far removed from the British equivalent. First World War German cemeteries often take the form of 'Heroes' Groves', mass graves in natural areas of beauty displaying no crosses or headstones. Often trees would be planted instead, symbolising the belief that the bodies would forever become part of the changing seasons. Jünger wrote in his seminal work, *Storm of Steel:*

> *The war had given the landscape a suggestion of heroism and melancholy.... The simple soul is convinced here that his life is deeply embedded in nature, and that his death is no end.*[9]

In *All Quiet on the Western Front,* Remarque comments how:

> *Those who still wear high boots tie sand bags round the top so that the mud does not pour in so fast. The rifles are caked, the uniforms caked, everything is fluid and dissolved, the earth one dripping, soaked, oily mass... Our hands are earth, our bodies' clay and our eyes pools of rain. We do not know whether we still live.*[10]

The death toll on the Western Front was so impossibly high that corpses would often lie out in No Man's Land, rotting in shell holes, or caught up in the wire, for weeks and months at a time. Those that could be salvaged would regularly be buried close to the trench lines, or in temporary cemeteries that were shelled as the lines moved or artillery ranges increased. Stories of equipment being hung on dismembered limbs poking through trench walls are not uncommon, as are more grisly tales of defensive

barricades built of corpses. The power of artillery gave rise to a new phenomenon, that of the 'missing'. This was the term given to those with no known grave, and there were almost as many of the missing as the known dead. Rarely before had there been nothing left at all of a soldier killed on the battlefield, but modern artillery rounds could reduce a man to little more than a pink mist. These unfortunate souls became nothing in an instant, blown to smithereens, their bodies mixing with the wind, the elements and the earth.

Rapidly, the Western Front became a place where the

living and the dead shared the same space and time. Men lived in the earth, died in the earth and were buried in the earth. As time passed, the destruction increased, seemingly exponentially, and the end appeared further away than ever before. The connections between soldiers and the fields of battle were so ambiguous that it was unclear as to whether the earth would protect or kill, and paradoxically the landscape that engulfed so many could also return them to the surface. Men who had been suddenly buried in an explosion could be 'rescued' from the ground by the next one, or pulled up from the slime to safety by comrades, resurrected: symbols of destruction and death turned to symbols of life and hope.[11]

FAR LEFT: We are Making a New World, Paul Nash Nash produced powerful and confident landscapes that were both visionary and terrifyingly realistic. His paintings show his outrage at the waste of life expressed through the violation of nature. (*Lebrecht Music & Arts*)

LEFT: Walter Kleinfeldt Nach Dem Sturm / After the Storm. Bodies strewn across the battlefield. (*bbc.co.uk*)

NACH DEM STURM

How could the natural world that was being destroyed so efficiently protect those guilty of its annihilation?

The First World War, then, fundamentally changed the long-held concepts of what form soldiers, wars and battlefields should take. The industrial necessity of modern warfare meant that conflict was now a battle of materiel, which inevitably gave rise to a myriad collection of objects through which many would come to understand events. It is fitting that the poppy first came to the attention of those immersed in the quagmire as early as 1915, perfectly capturing the fragile mix of life and landscape on the front lines. For many, the relationship between memory and the poppy stems from Lieutenant Colonel John McCrae's famous work, *In Flanders Fields*, a poem that inextricably linked the tangible and the intangible facets of modern warfare together in the common idiom. Nevertheless, the ambiguous connections between this small flower (along with its more potent cousins) and warfare can be traced far back into antiquity.[12] In other words, an emblem that has come to stand for the losses on the Western Front was already, at least to some degree, owned by the human cost of warfare centuries before 1914.

John McCrae was no stranger to conflict before he was sent to the Western Front. Born in Ontario on 30th November 1872, he had already flirted with poetry while a student. He received military training during the 1890s and when the South African war broke out in 1899, he volunteered and was commissioned, leading an artillery battery sourced from the town where he lived. The conflict brought home the horrors of war to McCrae and although he rose through the ranks, he resigned his commission in 1904, having tasted enough of war. Ten years later, he again volunteered along with almost fifty thousand other Canadians, and was appointed brigade-surgeon to the First Brigade of the Canadian Field Artillery, with the rank of Major. In April 1915, he was stationed near the Flemish town of Ypres (Ieper) and as the full force of this new type of warfare bombarded the trenches, he found himself in a land corrupted by the stench and feel of death. As the casualties mounted, one of McCrae's closest friends, Lieutenant Alexis Helmer, was killed. Another to add to so many that had gone before. The very next day, in his hastily written, yet eternal poem, he made the connection between the memory of the lost and the humble poppies that grew amongst their graves. Shortly after, McCrae was transferred to Dannes-Cammiers and not long after that the pressures of war began to affect him badly.

John McCrae.
(*Guelph Museums*)

**In Flanders Fields,
John McCrae**
First published in
England's *Punch*
magazine in
December 1915.
Within months,
this poem came
to symbolise the
sacrifices of all who
were fighting in the
First World War.
Today, the poem
continues to be
an abiding symbol
of remembrance
worldwide.

In Flanders Fields

—

In Flanders fields the poppies blow
Between the crosses, row on row,
That mark our place; and in the sky
The larks, still bravely singing, fly
Scarce heard amid the guns below.

We are the Dead. Short days ago
We lived, felt dawn, saw sunset glow,
Loved, and were loved, and now we lie
    In Flanders fields.

Take up our quarrel with the foe:
To you from failing hands we throw
The torch; be yours to hold it high.
If ye break faith with us who die
We shall not sleep, though poppies grow
    In Flanders fields

Punch
Dec 8 · 1915

John McCrae
—

His asthma, something he had coped with all his life, grew steadily worse, leading to a battle with bronchitis he would ultimately lose. Growing ever weaker, he died on 28 January 1918 and was buried in Wimereux Cemetery near Boulogne with full military honours.

In Flanders fields the poppies blow
Between the crosses, row on row,
That mark our place; and in the sky
The larks, still bravely singing, fly
Scarce heard amid the guns below.

We are the Dead. Short days ago
We lived, felt dawn, saw sunset glow,
Loved, and were loved, and now we lie
In Flanders fields.

Take up our quarrel with the foe:
To you from failing hands we throw
The torch, be yours to hold it high.
If ye break faith with us who die
We shall not sleep, though poppies grow
In Flanders fields

Australian poppy.

McCrae's poem not only perfectly encapsulates the human cost of modern warfare; it also embodies the notion that industrial conflict creates as it simultaneously destroys.[13]

The poppy is a hardy flower, one that grows well on shattered ground, mirroring how the present-day mirage of the Western Front has evolved over the past century. The moment the bells rang out on the eleventh hour of the eleventh month (and arguably even before that) the battle-zones began to change their character, develop and evolve. In Britain, tourists and pilgrims flocked to the Somme and Ypres to see the carnage for themselves or to seek out the last resting place of loved ones. Tours, and tour guides like those of the French company Michelin were created. The Englishman Thomas Cook started organizing trips from 1919 onwards, other companies were also created and soon this gave rise to tensions between pilgrims and tourists. The tourists had to be continuously reminded that they should show respect for the sites that they were visiting. At the same time, the bloodstained fields were being rapidly reclaimed. Cemeteries were formalised, shrouding the human cost of the conflict in a fog of loss, grief, reification and remembrance. Grand monuments, as well as the many Portland stone grave markers, became artefacts embedded

French machine-gun patrol in a trench overhung by poppies 1916. Autochrome by Jean-Baptiste Tournassoud. (Établissement Cinématographique et Photographique des Armées)

with the human experience of the war. Trench art sold to those who visited was often taken home and given pride of place in houses across Britain, forming a link between the missing, the lost and those they left behind.[14] In the battle-zones, while these changes took place, the poppy still grew, flourishing in the deeply shattered soil, its roots fed by the decomposing remains of so many. In Britain, the flower was soon to become another powerful object, one that directly linked man and nature together, reflecting how each was indistinguishable from one another on the front lines, both so ravaged by the power of modern weaponry and the brutality of twentieth-century 'civilisation'.

The start of the poppy's journey to a national symbol of remembrance began shortly before the end of the conflict and will be discussed in the next chapter, but notions of

Inauguration of the Menin Gate. *(Ryan Gearing)*

life rising from the mortuary landscape of the battlefields was a common theme after 1918. After attending the inauguration ceremony of the Menin Gate in Ypres, Will Longstaff, a veteran of the war, was so moved by what he witnessed that he embarked on his most famous work, *Menin Gate at Midnight*. His eerie canvas depicts the missing named on the imposing memorial rising out of the shattered, poppy-covered earth, mirroring the flower's phoenix-like ability.

Abel Gance's 1919 film, *J'accuse*, much of which was filmed before the end of the war on actual battlefields, undoubtedly influenced Longstaff. Gance's tale follows the dead *poilu* rising from the shattered ground, recycled by the carnage of war, to demand of the populace whether the conflict was worth the cost of their lives. Like the poppy, the evocative and emotional aspects of loss are often embodied in living things, born from the land of the dead. Throughout the war, the Germans shared a far greater connection with nature than their allied counterparts. It was not uncommon to find gardens directly behind the parados of German front line trenches. Vegetation was encouraged to grow and notes on how well it flourished were sent back to museums and other institutions in Germany.

Despite these connections, Germany has no official flower of remembrance, and in France it is the blue cornflower that is worn in memory of those who lost their lives. Even in Britain the remembrance poppy, seemingly omnipresent around November each year, was not a British invention, or even conceived by someone who had suffered directly as a result of the war. It was initially the idea of

Menin Gate at Midnight, Will Longstaff. Painted by Longstaff in a single session, today 'Menin Gate at Midnight' has achieved the status of an international icon commemorating those soldiers with no marked graves on the Western Front during the First World War, also known as 'Ghosts of Menin Gate'. (*Australian War Memorial*)

an American, and later taken up by a Frenchwoman. Like so many of the artefacts associated with the conflict, the remembrance poppy was created because of this war of matériel, reflecting life in the earth, an object recycled and given new meaning by the changing nature of conflict in the early twentieth century.

But the question must be asked, why the poppy, and not any of the other flowers that grew amongst the bloodshed? The common belief of the entire Western Front being a sea of mud is far from the truth. For the British, the most intense areas of fighting – the Ypres Salient, Vimy, the Labyrinth and much of the Somme front – were eventually reduced to quagmires loaded with the industrial detritus of war, indeed becoming the archetypal First World War battlefields of legend. But in areas where the fighting was less severe, and even at different times of year in places where it was not, the front line could look very different. Private Len Smith, who served with the London Regiment, like so many others kept a record of his time in France.[15] In his diary, Smith drew many colourful images of what he saw. The collection contains several drawings modern observers would recognise as battlefields, but he also drew the front line covered in grass (even around places long-associated with mud and misery, such as Vimy Ridge). Pictures of buttercups and fruit bushes also feature, as do sketches of sniper suits – green sniper suits covered in

leaves, twigs and bushes, not mud, chalk and dirt. Not only could the front line appear peaceful at times, but also, more generally, the surrounding land only a short distance away from the firing line could seem completely unblemished to those who visited it. This offered soldiers entombed in their trenches the occasional tantalising view of normality – a phenomenon played upon by Charles Sims in his painting *The Old German Frontline, Arras, 1916*.

In part, what differentiated the poppy from the other flora that grew in the battle-zones was that it already had a place in history as a flower of remembrance, and its connections to morphine, the drug of dreams, were already well established.[16] To educated men, and particularly a doctor like McCrae, these links would have added to the allure of the poppy as an object that embodied the agency of war and the new world being forged at the front. In the British ranks soldiers spent only a few days at a time in the trenches. The High Command quickly realised the advantages of troop rotation, yet those days could consist of total boredom, or frequent terror and discomfort. When times were difficult, how tempting it must have been for soldiers to relate to the poppy, a bright flower, so associated with pain relief, which could do much to alleviate their discomfort, thereby distorting the already warped reality they found themselves in. Rum and cigarettes may have eased the burdens of combat, but the poppy's gifts could do so much more. Of course, much of this may have been little more than wishful thinking, but it cannot have escaped many that the murdered earth claiming so many men could also produce such beauty and the promise of mental nirvana. The bond between soldiers and the earth they lived in became stronger and stronger as the war's violence escalated. As more of the battle-zones fell victim to high explosive, and men dug ever deeper to escape its wrath, the notion of the grey earth offering life would give hope to many.

References

1. Jünger, E. (2004). *Storm of Steel.* London: Penguin Classics. P 41.
2. Masefield, J. (2003). *The Old Frontline.* Barnsley: Pen and Sword Military Classics. P 107.
3. Das, S. (2008). *Touch and Intimacy in First World War Literature.* Cambridge: Cambridge University Press.
4. Das, S. (2008). *Touch and Intimacy in First World War Literature.* Cambridge: Cambridge University Press. P 45.
5. Das, S. (2008). *Touch and Intimacy in First World War Literature.* Cambridge: Cambridge University Press. P 35.
6. Carpenter, H. (1977). *J. R. R. Tolkien: A Biography.* London: George Allen & Unwin Ltd. P 84.
7. Carpenter, H. (ed). (1995). *The Letters of J. R. R. Tolkien.* London: Houghton Mifflin. P 303.
8. Tolkien, J. R. R. (2008). *The Two Towers (The Lord of The Rings Vol. II).* London: Harper Collins. P 820.
9. Jünger, E. (2004). *Storm of Steel.* London: Penguin Classics. P 143.
10. Remarque, E. (1929). *All Quiet on the Western Front.* Little Brown. Boston. P 283-284.
11. Mosse, G. (1990). *Fallen Soldiers: Reshaping the Memory of the World Wars.* New York: Oxford University Press. P 108.
12. Saunders, N. J. (2013). *The Poppy: A Cultural History from Ancient Egypt to Flanders Fields and Afghanistan.* London: Oneworld. P 25.
13. Saunders, N. J. (2004). 'Material Culture and Conflict: The Great War, 1914-2003.' In N. J. Saunders. (ed.). *Matters of Conflict: Material Culture, Memory and the First World War.* Abingdon: Routledge. P 5.
14. Saunders, N. J. (2004). 'Material Culture and Conflict: The Great War, 1914-2003.' In N. J. Saunders. (ed.). *Matters of Conflict: Material Culture, Memory and the First World War.* Abingdon: Routledge. P 15.
15. Smith, L. (2009). *Drawing Fire.* London: Collins.
16. Saunders, N, J. (2013). *The Poppy: A Cultural History from Ancient Egypt to Flanders Fields and Afghanistan.* London: Oneworld. Pp 41-66.

A History of the Remembrance Poppy

When the human cost of the First World War is fully considered, it's perhaps strange that the idea of a remembrance flower didn't come from someone bereaved by the conflict, or even a citizen of one of the major belligerent nations. Moina Belle Michael was born in Good Hope, Georgia on 15th August 1869. Although her parents were American citizens, her family history could be traced back to Belgian Flanders and France, the major

Moina Belle Michael.
Presenting a copy of her story of the Flanders Fields Poppy 'The Miracle Flower' in 1941. (*Special Collections and Archives, Georgia State University Library*)

British theatres of the conflict. America's entry into the war came late, and her first combat involvement even later. Nevertheless, in September 1918, Michael decided that she would leave her teaching job and do her bit for the war effort. By that time the United States had been losing men on the European battlefields for less than six months, but many in the homeland were well aware of the price being paid in blood to enter this 'World War'. Moina Michael was one of them and for her reading about the conflict from such a great distance was not enough, so she applied for a YMCA training course teaching young women to become Overseas War Secretaries (OWS). Despite her obvious abilities, as well as passing the course, at fifty-nine she was deemed too old to travel to Europe, so she settled instead for a role at the OWS head office.

On 9th November 1918, Michael was waiting in a meeting room at the OWS offices to speak to a delegate visiting as part of the organisation's 25th anniversary celebrations when she glanced at the latest issue of the *Ladies' Home Journal,* and saw an image of fallen soldiers emerging from their graves juxtaposed with McCrae's poem.[1] The effect it had on her was spiritual, almost other-worldly, and although she had read the poem before, the combination of symbolism, poetry and the still-burning desire to be more directly involved in the war effort, led her to embark on her life's work; the creation of the remembrance poppy.

As Saunders notes, the feelings sparked by the imagery encouraged her to reach for pen and paper, and write the following words in response to McCrae's final stanza:

Take up our quarrel with the foe;
To you from failing hands we throw
The torch; be yours to hold it high.
If ye break faith with us who die
We shall not sleep, though poppies grow
In Flanders fields.[2]

Royal British Legion's
Paper Poppy.

This she followed with a poem of her own:

Oh! You who sleep in Flanders' fields,
Sleep sweet – to rise anew,
We caught the torch you threw,
And holding high we kept
The faith with those who died.
We cherish too, the poppy red
That grows on fields where valour led.
It seems to signal to the skies
That blood of heroes never dies.
But lends a lustre to the red
Of the flower that blooms above the dead
In Flanders' fields.
And now the torch and poppy red

POPPYGANDA

Wear in honour of our dead.
Fear not that ye have died for naught
We've learned the lesson that ye taught
In Flanders' fields.[3]

These lines were to set Michael on a journey that would change her life. Several of the OWS delegates read her poem and, moved by her words, gave her money to buy flowers to brighten up the office. With poetry still flowing through her mind she spent the money on red poppies, declaring that 'I shall always wear red poppies – poppies of Flanders Fields'.[4] With no fresh flowers available, she purchased silk ones instead and handed all but one, which she kept for herself, over to the delegates. It was the first time that poppies had been bought with donated money in the memory of those who had died in the war. The timing was fortuitous, as two days later the conflict ended, finally closing the door on more than four years of bloodshed, and simultaneously opening another into an uncharted world of mass remembrance and grief, for which the poppy would become a defining symbol.

Michael had found her calling in life. Inspired by McCrae's words, she called for the poppy to be worn in memory of those Americans killed in Flanders. Her quest brought her into contact with Lee Keedick, head of a speaker's agency in New York. Keedick was about to visit Europe, and realising the potential of the poppy, he immediately entered into an agreement with Michael to campaign for her cause. It's often said that objects have a social life all of their own and that from this life they garner their worth. The poppy is no exception and here the tale of the this flower took a strange turn. Feeling that the simplicity of the poppy might turn off potential adoptees, Keedick changed the powerful symbol into a 'Torch of Liberty' reducing the poppy to a sideshow. The new emblem was a confused mix of national flags, the Torch of Liberty and the poppy, devaluing the power of McCrae's words and imagery. The 'Flanders Victory Memorial Flag', as the new emblem was christened, was quickly dismissed and soon Michael returned home to try and set the poppy back in its rightful place. Alas, disappointment followed, and try as she might she couldn't build up a head of steam, until that is she attended a convention run by the Georgia branch of the American Legion. There she tirelessly lobbied for the Legion to adopt her beloved poppy, and succeeded in obtaining a promise that every 11th November the Legion would wear the flower in memory of American troops that had perished. These small victories not only placed the poppy's journey towards infamy back on track, but also led to it becoming internationally recognised.

In 1920, the Georgia branch of the Legion promoted the poppy at the national convention in Ohio with great success. The American Legion was seduced and the poppy was voted in as their emblem of remembrance. In the audience was a Frenchwoman named Anna Guérin, a kindred spirit of Michael's who would help propel the poppy to world renown, although the path would not be a smooth one. Guérin had already been promoting the poppy in France, creating silk flowers to be worn in remembrance, but her goal was to produce them by the million, not the dozen. A visit to America in 1919 brought Guérin in contact with the Legion, who proclaimed her the 'Poppy Lady of France'[5] and after being lobbied by two women passionate about the flower's potential, the Legion gave their full approval for a remembrance poppy. Guérin's plan was to manufacture the silk poppies in France and then sell them to the American Legion. The proceeds would then go to the French war-widows who made them,

A 1921 Poppy as adopted by the British Legion with original label, 'Made by the women and children in the devastated areas of France'. (*James Brazier*)

Official Poppy Seller tag from 1923. (*James Brazier*)

and the Legion could use the funds earned from selling the flowers to the public to benefit America's wounded and widowed citizens.

Guérin didn't stop with America. Her ambitions were global, and helped by Sir Douglas Haig, who was deeply touched by the remembrance poppy, the British Legion adopted the flower for their own appeal fund. For the first poppy day to be held in Britain, in 1921, Guérin received an order for some nine million flowers, which were exchanged for a voluntary donation, reaping in more than £106,000 for the Legion.[6] The

Poppy Day, Margate 11 November 1922 six days after the unveiling of the war memorial. How many of the children gathered in this photograph had lost their fathers just years before? (*Margate Civic Society*)

POPPYGANDA

ability of the flower to touch the hearts of millions was now obvious, but Guérin's success had a downside. Soon it was suggested that poppies sold in Britain should be made by British soldiers wounded in the conflict, depriving Guérin's war-widows of their income. The motion was passed and a factory promptly opened in Richmond, Surrey. The decision may have been to the detriment of the French, but it was to the gain of the English. In 1922 over 30 million poppies were ordered, a number that brought in double the revenue from the previous year.[7]

Despite the loss of income from Britain, Guérin was undeterred in her efforts. She soon recruited Australia, New Zealand and Canada to her cause. But Guérin was becoming a victim of her own success and the staggering

For over 90 years, the Poppy Factory in Richmond, Surrey, has been making poppies, crosses and wreaths for The Royal Family and The Royal British Legion's Poppy Appeal.
(*Ian Paterson*)

A volunteer constructs poppies at the Royal British Legion Poppy Factory, Richmond, Surrey where over 30 million Poppies are made by a small team each year. (© *Crown copyright 2007*)

BELOW AND RIGHT: As in the United States and Canada, the British poppies were made during the first year by Anna Guérin's organisation for women and children in the devastated areas of France. Shortly afterwards, in 1922, Major George Howson set up the Poppy Factory in Richmond, where disabled war veterans were employed. The centre of the British poppies displayed the Haig Fund imprint until 1994. (*James Brazier*)

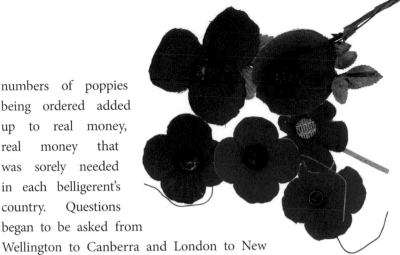

numbers of poppies
being ordered added
up to real money,
real money that
was sorely needed
in each belligerent's
country. Questions
began to be asked from
Wellington to Canberra and London to New
York about the wisdom of the French profiting from
the remembrance poppy, and soon each nation decided to
make their own versions, thereby benefitting their own war-
weary. Despite their different approaches, both Michael and
Guérin ensured that the poppy would become the defining
symbol of remembrance amongst many of the Allied
nations, but the two women fared very differently in the eyes
of history. Michael published *The Miracle Flower* in 1941,
thereby cementing forever her association with the poppy,
and Guérin eventually faded into obscurity, leaving Michael
to take the plaudits. Awards became a frequent occurrence,
a Liberty ship was named after her, and her original vision of
the remembrance poppy even appeared on a postage stamp.[8]

The poppy seemed to perfectly encapsulate the purpose
for which it was chosen. It is a flower that grows on
shattered ground with ease and one that seemed to carpet

the immolated surface of the Western Front even while the fighting still raged. Today, in the twenty-first century, the poppy still holds the public in its memorial grasp. Each year these small paper flowers are left in their thousands across the former battle-zones of Europe and beyond. Many are placed by relatives at the grand memorials to the missing at such places as Thiepval, Ypres, Vimy and the heights of the Gallipoli peninsular. Remembrance gardens crop up around November with increasing regularity and schools ask children to plant real poppies to teach them about the cost of war. Every year during the Festival of Remembrance in the Royal Albert Hall the audience are showered with poppy petals and many other similar ceremonies take place across the world with the flower as the centrepiece. Over the coming years the poppy will only grow in stature as the world remembers the hundred year anniversary of the conflict's beginning, middle and end, no doubt reaching levels that could scarcely have been imagined by Michael and Guérin, but ones of which they would certainly be proud. Whether or not they would feel the same way about the way that other organisations have purloined their beloved symbol of remembrance is another matter. An object as successful as the poppy was always going to be appropriated for other purposes; it was an inevitable stage in its biography.

The very reason the poppy became so prevalent was

Langemarck German Military Cemetery, Flanders. In the foreground is an inscription on a flat stone with a sculpted wreath. This records the 44,061 men buried here. Ahead of the sculpted wreath is the mass grave of nearly 25,000 men. At the rear is the lifesize bronze statue of four mourning soldiers, by the Munich sculptor Professor Emil Krieger. (*Shutterstock*)

because the war-dead were legion and their numbers could not be hidden. This inevitably cemented the dead in the public consciousness at the expense of the living. Before the conflict had ended those who had fallen in battle began to be reified, giving birth to what George Mosse termed 'the cult of the fallen soldier'.[9] According to Mosse, the notion of the dead as being somehow resurrected through their sacrifice was a necessary construct if the armies at the front were to continue to be fed with manpower.

In Germany this myth can be traced back to the Battle of Langemarck in 1914, when regiments consisting of 'youths and volunteers' stormed the English lines and were shot down in their thousands, while allegedly singing the *Deutschlandlied* as they 'willingly' gave their lives for the Fatherland. The image took hold of young boys becoming men as they fell to the enemy guns, sparking a raft of poetry and prose idolising their sacrifice and elevating them to the status of Greek heroes.[10] That less than eighteen percent of those in the German regiments at Langemarck were students didn't matter. Nor did the fact that the battle wasn't fought at Langemarck at all, but at nearby Bixchote, some five kilometres to the west. Langemarck sounded more Germanic, and youths hurling themselves at the enemy's guns for love of the Fatherland was intensely evocative, personal and patriotic. The myth took hold. The brave German dead were buried in Heroes' Groves where their bodies could be reintegrated back into nature, giving them an eternal presence and amalgamating them with the natural world. As Mosse put it, 'death was no longer conceived as the arrival of the Grim Reaper, but as a tranquil sleep within nature.'[11] In Britain, Belgium and France similar, albeit less Germanic, steps were being taken to achieve the same ends, but in these countries it was the construction of grand memorials and picturesque cemeteries that allowed the myth to really take hold.

France enshrined the concept of a military cemetery in law as early as 1914, England was close behind and in September 1915 Germany's Ministry of War instructed that war graves should be permanently cared for. British

Field of Remembrance at the Menin Gate, Ypres, 2011. *(Ryan Gearing)*

cemeteries would be centred on the Cross of Sacrifice and Kipling's protestation that 'Their name liveth for evermore' further focused the attention of the living on the dead. The construction in the years immediately after the war of the Menin Gate at Ypres, the Memorial to the Missing at Thiepval and the grand ossuaries and cemeteries at Notre Dame de Lorette and Douaumont raised the bar again. Yet, in these countries were thousands of men who had survived the war, often horribly maimed, either physically or mentally by what they had experienced. For many, the sight of so many poppies every November, often worn by politicians, the very same people perceived by the public (not always fairly) to have avoided the front while sending others to their fate, was too much. It appeared that the poppy, a symbol of the soldier's relationship with nature and modern warfare, was being used to glorify military might rather than remember the dead.

Military power may have brought victory, but the misery, loss and grief that came with it was a price many thought too high. Pacifism, as well as membership of movements and societies opposed to war, increased in popularity, helped no end by the patronage of the rich and famous. In 1926, it was suggested that one of these organisations, the No More War movement, should adopt the white poppy as its symbol, and the seed was planted. In the years immediately after 1918, victory was loudly celebrated every year around Armistice Day. Yet it didn't take long for the many balls, parties and dinners (along with the occasional drinking hours extension) that celebrated the war to become increasingly seen as vulgar, and this coupled with the over-militaristic Remembrance Day ceremonies drove many to the pacifist's table. In 1925 a victory ball in the Royal Albert Hall was postponed and two years later the first British Legion Festival of Remembrance took place at the same venue.[12] Articles and letters in the national press urged the public to oppose all future wars and within the space of two years more than 100,000 had signed up to membership of the Peace Pledge Union, a new group dedicated to the cessation of conflict, which could boast the likes of Vera Britten, Aldous Huxley and Siegfried Sassoon as members.[13]

It was another of the pacifist movements that first subverted the remembrance poppy. The British Women's Co-operative Guild had been in existence since 1883. Originally it was set up to defend Victorian family values, but since 1914 it had vociferously opposed the war. In 1933, after seeing the power the remembrance poppy wielded, the Guild created its own version – the white poppy. Even though the Guild insisted the white poppy should not be seen as an alternative to the red one, rather as a complimentary symbol that at the same time stood for an end to war and the memory of those affected by it, the Guild were playing with fire. The British Legion refused to acknowledge the symbol, but that didn't diminish its growing popularity. By 1937, sales of white poppies hit 85,000 and by the start of the Second World War the number was even higher. Even so, many veterans saw the white poppy as something of an insult. It echoed memories of the white feather handed out to contentious objectors, or flags waved in surrender.[14] After 1945 the white poppy ebbed and flowed in its popularity and even today is still often viewed with suspicion. But in terms of the poppy as a powerful symbol, red and white are not the only colours. Black poppies have been used to bring attention to problems of world hunger and in 2014 counter-militarism

A white poppy derived from the Women's Co-operative Guild 'a pledge to peace that war must not happen again.'

activists plastered 16,000 posters representing conscientious objectors from the First World War across Glasgow in an act to re-politicise the symbol of remembrance to respect people's right to resist. Purple poppies are distributed every year by Animal Aid and worn to highlight the terrible damage done to animals in times of war; the golden poppy is the official state flower of California.

But what of the other nations involved in the conflict? Over three million poppies are sent abroad each year from Britain to over 120 countries as far-flung as France, Spain, Germany, Kazakhstan, Sri Lanka and Argentina. Although most are worn by ex-pats, many in the local communities embrace them, too. South Africa has seen a growth in poppy wearing during November each year. Scotland also has its own poppy that sports four petals and not two. Millions of poppies are distributed every year in Canada and the same applies to New Zealand, although poppy day there falls on the Friday in April before ANZAC Day. Malawi even receives a batch annually.

Despite the success of the flower in so many places, it was not taken up with such passion everywhere. In Northern Ireland the poppy remains a divisive symbol closely linked to

Purple poppies distributed by Animal Aid.

Canadian poppy.

Remembrance poppy of
New Zealand.

subservience to the British monarchy. For the
people of Northern Ireland, the poppy recalls
the heights which sectarianism reached in the late
1980s. On Remembrance Day in 1987 a huge bomb
was detonated near the Enniskillen cenotaph.[15] Many
people were injured and 11 lost their lives. To many, the
poppy now has a contested image; to some it will be forever
associated with the Great War in which Irishmen of all
faiths and political persuasions fought and died together.
To others it is inextricably linked to the breakdown of that
'togetherness', bringing death to those who remembered
the death of others. Despite the myriad connotations,
the remembrance poppy has undergone something of
a resurgence in Northern Ireland during recent years;
perhaps the grief that surrounds the flower has the power to
settle modern political differences without the bloodshed
it represents.

American Legion
Poppy. Hand
made and sold by
veterans today
since 1924.

In the USA, the red poppy, or at least Michael's version of
it, remains the official remembrance flower, but it is obscure
to many modern Americans. Most, if they sport any emblem
on Remembrance Day at all,
prefer to wear a red, white
and blue ribbon, an object
more in keeping with American patriotic values.
America's late entry into the war didn't stop her losing
over 170,000 men, yet it is the Second World War that is

THE AMERICAN LEGION
AMERICAN LEGION AUXILIARY
HAND-MADE BY VETERANS

Remembrance wreath. In the USA it is more common for Remembrance Day to be marked with a red, white and blue ribbon. (*Shutterstock*)

'Veterans of Foreign Wars' Poppy. The VFW conducted its first poppy distribution in the USA in 1922. (*VFW*)

given preference in the collective memory, by-passing the inherent links between the poppy, static battlefields and mass casualties. Memory is an elusive concept and rarely straightforward in its visual representation – up until very recently there was no official First World War memorial in America. Her late entry into the conflict was a source of shame for some, and to some extent this is reflected in the country's reticence to engage with the flower to the same extent as her European allies. The experiences of Vietnam did little to enhance the poppy's remembrance values, with most, if linking the flower with that conflict at all, drawing parallels with morphine and the drug problems experienced by the military's often unwillingly conscripted civilian soldiers. The conflict divided America, and many returning soldiers were vilified by sections of the public. According to veteran Jack Sturiano, the Veterans of Foreign Wars and the American Legion could have done more for those coming back to the States, even frowning on the fact that these men only had to serve one-year combat tours – not like during the Second World War when soldiers fought on until the job was done. The recent experiences

in Iraq and Afghanistan further cloud things, as does the notion that poppies tend to be worn on Memorial Day (traditionally the last Sunday in May) as opposed to during November. Nevertheless, remembrance poppies in the United States still regularly garner donations of around $2m, showing that to some at least it is still the true flower of remembrance.

For their part, the French never took the poppy to their hearts, preferring the blue cornflower (*le bleuet*) instead. Its bright hue is representative of the uniforms that replaced the red-trouser ensemble worn by the French in the early stages of the war; a sartorial change that became a symbol for the way the conflict shattered the innocent attitudes to modern war. The cornflower shares many similarities with the poppy. Both grow on disturbed land, and both were often seen growing side by side on the Western Front. As with the poppy, the remembrance cornflower has its roots in the maimed and injured of the war, yet the journey from flower to object of memory is perhaps more direct.

(*Jules Michel Chartier*)

Suzane Lenhardt was head nurse at Les Invalides in Paris, and someone well accustomed to grief – her husband Maurice, an infantry captain, had been killed on 3rd February 1915. While working at the hospital she met Charlotte Malleterre, the daughter of the institution's Commander-in-Chief, and together they devised a scheme to occupy the minds of those recuperating. The first remembrance cornflowers consisted of fabric petals and stamens made of newspaper, and were only sold locally in Paris, but in 1928, President Doumergue patronised the *le bleuet*, giving it much wider recognition. Revenues from sales brought those who made them a small stipend and gradually the remembrance cornflower became a symbol of the rehabilitation of the *poilu* through work. After the war, it was apparent that thousands of men were to be discharged from the army into a life of poverty, so the production of the remembrance cornflower was formalised. Workshops were created and cornflower badges were made from tissue paper, as opposed to fabric, increasing production while lowering costs, thereby increasing the income to be made, considerably. The organisation became known as *Le Bleuet de France* and in recent times the French Government has lent its support, enabling continued benefits for many veterans and their families.

For Britain and the Commonwealth, Belgium, France and America, the way that the dead were remembered was certainly influenced by victory – those deemed to have paid the ultimate price to secure the world from German aggression were to be celebrated and remembered. In

Germany, things were very different. Not only had she lost the war, she had lost vast swathes of territory, as well as at least two million dead, and would now face the bill for the entire conflagration. There was no room for the emergence of a memorial object akin to the remembrance poppy. Since 1945, Germany has further distanced herself from the wars that cost her so dear. The British are the main visitors to German cemeteries on the Western Front. To Germans, the First World War resonates of rampant militarism, a state of affairs far removed from present-day attitudes. So little attention is paid to the conflict and those who served that when Erich Kaestner, Germany's last veteran, died in 2008 at the age of 107, barely a line was written in the

President Hollande of France after a special Last Post Ceremony in Ypres, commemorating 100 years since the First World War. The ceremony signalled the start of a two-day EU summit which was also attended by British Prime Minister David Cameron and German chancellor Angela Merkel. (*Dominiek Dendooven*) national press. The government didn't even confirm he was the final veteran – there are no official records in existence. Compare this to the attitudes in Britain to the death of Harry Patch, or in France to the death of Lazare Ponticelli, who received a state funeral when at one hundred and ten he became the last of the *poilu* to die.

Despite its sombre connotations, the poppy has not been able to avoid the commercialisation of remembrance. Museums from Flanders to the Somme, along with many in the UK, bedeck their gift shops with all manner of poppy memorabilia. The variations on the theme are staggering; ranging from T-shirts to umbrellas, posters to badges, books to DVDs, wristbands to seeds. In the small town of Ypres (Ieper), a place that arguably depends on the very thing that almost destroyed it for commercial survival, the situation is even more pronounced. Chocolatiers' windows display all manner of edible poppies, now even available in the correct colours. In many bars a 'poppy beer' can be found. Bed and breakfasts, along with holiday apartments, school hostels and battlefield tour operators all lean heavily on the poppy, adopting its name or image to draw in tourists. Until recently there was even a 'Poppies' restaurant within sight of the Menin Gate. Even while

Poppies Gin to remember the fallen in the Ypres Salient.
(Ryan Gearing)

POPPYGANDA

Selection of poppy merchandise recently displayed at the In Flanders Fields Museum, Ypres.
(*Ryan Gearing*)

the remembrance poppy was in its infancy it had already become a tool of propaganda. Appropriated by different organisations, nationalities and individuals, subverted from its original design, and purloined as a marketing device. It was a pattern that was to continue and one that shows little sign of abating.

From the perspective of the twenty-first century it is difficult to consider the First World War without simultaneously thinking of the poppy. In this regard, the wishes of Michael and Guérin have been fulfilled. Even so, the commercial success of this remembrance flower must bear some responsibility for the way the war is now perceived. The human cost of the Western Front has long been hidden under a carpet of little red petals, but the biography of the poppy has also contributed to the re-working of the war's history. As we shall see in the next chapter, the fields of Flanders, the Artois and the Somme now carry little resemblance to the way they were almost a hundred years ago, and the poppy had a prominent role to play in this re-creation.

The triennial meeting place of bubbling cat folklore in Ypres, the Cat Festival 'Kattenstoet' culminates with the 'King and Queen Cat' parading. The Queen, Minneke Poes wearing a grand Poppy costume. (*Ryan Gearing*)

References

1. Saunders, N. J. (2013). *The Poppy: A Cultural History from Ancient Egypt to Flanders Fields and Afghanistan.* London: Oneworld. P 97.

2. *Ibid:* P 98.

3. *Ibid:* P 99.

4. *Ibid:* P 100.

5. *Ibid:* P 105.

6. *Ibid:* P 107.

7. *Ibid:* P 110.

8. *Ibid:* P 124.

9. Mosse, G. (1990). *Fallen Soldiers: Reshaping the Memory of the World Wars.* New York: Oxford University Press. Pp 70-106.

10. *Ibid:* P 73.

11. *Ibid:* P 80.

12. Saunders, N. J. (2013). *The Poppy: A Cultural History from Ancient Egypt to Flanders Fields and Afghanistan.* London: Oneworld. Pp 158-159.

13. *Ibid:* P 159

14. Saunders, N. J. (2013). *The Poppy: A Cultural History from Ancient Egypt to Flanders Fields and Afghanistan.* London: Oneworld. P 164.

15. *Ibid:* P 215.

The Twenty-first Century Western Front

Today, the Western Front is a place where the trauma of the past contests the legacy of the future. Even though tens of thousands visit the former battlefields every year, there is relatively little to see in terms of trenches, dug outs, shell holes, barbed wire and the other accoutrements of war. Instead there is a carefully crafted version of the conflict, one that prioritises the dead over the living and isolates moments in time for preservation at the expense of others. The remembrance poppy embodies much of this visage in its carefully sculpted paper petals.

Poppies on the Somme near Beaumont Hamel. (*Author*)

Sanctuary Wood.
A recreated section
of trenches near
Ypres.
(*Ryan Gearing*)

For those of us who have never experienced combat, and perhaps even for some that have, the wartime landscape of the Western Front is almost impossible to imagine. John Masefield's *The Old Frontline* vividly describes the Somme in 1916 after the British lines had finally moved forward, yet even the words of a poet laureate don't do justice to the sheer desolation. The German soldier Ernst Jünger described the scene at the time in one area as:

> *The defile proved to be little more than a series of enormous craters full of pieces of uniform, weapons and dead bodies; the country around, so far as the eye could see, had been completely ploughed by heavy shells. Not a single blade of grass showed itself. The churned-up field was gruesome. In among the living defenders lay the dead. When we dug foxholes, we*

realized that they were stacked in layers. One company after another, pressed together in the drumfire, had been mown down, then the bodies had been buried under showers of earth sent up by shells. And then the relief company had taken their predecessor's place. And now it was our turn.[1]

Sassoon's imagery was just as rich, picturing a captured German trench as:

Wrecked as though by earthquake and eruption. Concrete strong-posts were smashed and tilted sideways; everywhere the chalky soil was pocked and pitted with huge shell-holes; and wherever we looked the mangled effigies of the dead were our memento mori.[2]

Poppy memorabilia, crystal poppy earrings.
(Ryan Gearing)

The pre-war landscape had been savaged by industrial firepower, but after 1918 this tortured place retreated to the shadows surprisingly quickly. Even so, the lethal legacy of modern war still festered beneath the metal-infused soil and is destined to do so for many years to come. As people returned home and farmers began to reclaim their lands many were killed or injured coming into contact with the tonnes of unexploded ordnance that still carpeted the earth. Even today, the dangers still exist – in March 2014 two construction workers were killed in Ypres while inspecting an unearthed shell,

'Iron Harvest.'
(*Ryan Gearing*)

Circuit of Remembrance.
(*Author*)

and the infamous 'Iron Harvest' still annually extracts its toll. To the British, the Somme, Flanders and the remembrance poppy are inextricably linked. Of course, to many, the baking torture of the Dardanelles campaign, the terror of the Atlantic convoys, or the arid wastelands of Mesopotamia also loom large. Yet, overwhelmingly, tour operators, authors, television programmes, historians, archaeologists and the millions who wear the poppy every year focus on these overtly 'British' battlefields in Europe, unconsciously marginalising the years of fighting that rumbled on elsewhere in nameless and forgotten places. Many who visit the Somme follow the *Circuit of Remembrance*, a route across the battle-zone that takes in museums, cemeteries, monuments and notorious areas of fighting. Signposts proudly display the poppy, ensuring they stand out from the crowd, lending verisimilitude to the places they direct tourists to. Literature on the subject in this part of France brazenly states the poppy is 'a flower of the Somme', laying claim to the contested object from the outset. Gift shops across the region (and elsewhere) sell poppy-branded goods in every conceivable form; umbrellas, chocolates, T-shirts, key rings, books, wristbands, stationery, cufflinks, crockery, posters, postcards, badges, pins, dresses, bags, rings, bracelets, watches, necklaces, ear-rings, wallets, jackets, phone cases, teddy bears, faux medals, stickers, towels, bedding, bottle-openers....

This symbol of remembrance is now also a symbol of the commercial reality of today's Western Front. With so many visitors there is too much money to be made, too many opportunities to be had, and too many temptations to tell one version of events at the expense of another. For much of the route taken through the Somme and Flanders all there is to see are fields, countryside, cemeteries and isolated memorials, amongst which, of course, the poppy blooms. Almost all of the 'sights' favour the British, and occasionally French, version of events. The poppy acts as a badge of legitimacy, assuring visitors of the 'truths' of what they see. But what is really seen?

The Somme's farmland was far too valuable to the economy (both local and national) to be left as a decaying battle-zone, so trenches were back-filled, dugout and tunnel entrances were blown in, and the former front lines either cleared of detritus, or sealed off and labelled as too dangerous to reclaim, creating a fresh canvas on which to paint the history of the conflict. In a few short years a swathe of northern France and Belgium changed from a landscape of war to one of memory and ritual remembrance, contesting space with the other violent legacies of twentieth century conflict. The mass graves and cemeteries that populate the area reinforce the huge loss of life suffered on the Somme. As early as 1917, Sir Edwin

Serre Road No. 2 Cemetery designed by Sir Edwin Lutyens. The largest on the Somme and enlarged after the Armistice to include graves from the surrounding area. It was not completed until 1934. (*Ryan Gearing*)

Lutyens described the battlefield in a letter to his wife: 'the graveyards, haphazard from the needs of much to do and little time for thought. And then a ribbon of isolated graves like a milky way across miles of country where men were tucked where they fell.'[3] By 1934, in the Somme region alone 150,000 British and Commonwealth dead had been buried in 242 cemeteries, and in total 918 cemeteries were built on the Western Front, draped over the blood-soaked fields. By the late 1930s much of this new layer was complete on the British parts of the front and, apart from some notable exceptions, little has been added to it since.

The sense of place has been distorted by this change in the landscape. Coupled with the magnitude of the events on the Somme, this has left a confused place that in many ways struggles for a clear identity. The Somme was the scene of terrible fighting for most of the war, not just the bloody year of 1916. Two years later the British relinquished much of the hard won ground, only to recapture it a few months after that. Thiepval, Beaumont Hamel, Warlencourt and La Boisselle, to name a few, are places frozen in time, forever to be associated with July 1916, regardless of the role they did or didn't play. Trench warfare and long-range artillery enabled the same stretch of land to be fought over for years, so much so that the idea of preserving a 1916 area of the battlefield, however noble the intention, is illusionary.[4] The Somme is grounded in a bewildered palimpsest of time, some events chosen over others and many neglected altogether. It is right and proper that so many dead should be remembered, but despite the terrible loss of life, less than 20 percent of those in the British ranks that attacked on 1st July 1916 were killed. Almost 30,000 were wounded and

A lone poppy on the Thiepval monument. (*Simon Gregor*)

Poppies mark relatives' names on the panels of the Menin Gate Memorial, Ypres. *(Ryan Gearing)*

over 50,000 came through 'physically unscathed'. The sculpted history visible today prioritises the dead over the living. Visitors to battlefields weep in the cemeteries, and guides are constantly asked to regurgitate the numbers of dead, thereby revealing figures that most can make little sense of. The living and undamaged, if there was such a thing, along with the brutally disfigured wounded, are forgotten. These men clambered out of trenches and stinking shell holes along with those who perished, only by chance avoiding the murderous fire. The living and the dead were as brave as each other, both contributed to the eventual successes on the Somme, and successes they were. By the time the battle was brought to a close in November 1916 the back of the German army had been broken and Verdun was saved. Not until mid-1918 would Germany be capable of attacking en masse, and by then it was far too late, yet the Somme feels like a defeat, a place where heads should be bowed, voices should be kept to a whisper, and minds befuddle at the 'waste of human life'. There is almost no attention at all paid to those that survived, or that few, if any, of those who perished represented 'wasted lives'.

One of the reasons for this is scale. The statistics are simply staggering. The number of dead, the number of wounded, the amount of shells fired, bullets expended, mines detonated, horses killed, food and water consumed, the length of the battle and many other difficult to comprehend figures all contribute to the statistical mire. Together, they create an image difficult to process, let alone understand. When these numbers are added to claims of men walking slowly into machine gun fire, often described by the sombre voices of guides or television presenters, it is little surprise that the human psyche becomes fixated with

Poppy wreaths at the stone of remembrance, Lijssenthoek Military Cemetery, home to almost 11,000 fallen represeting 30 nationalities. (*Ryan Gearing*)

the dead. In many cemeteries remembrance poppies are left on or by headstones. At the Menin Gate, Tyne Cot and other shrines to the missing these little paper flowers are placed next to names engraved on the walls and plaques, or left in wreaths leant against the foot of regimental memorials. On Remembrance Day every year the base of the Lochnagar crater is covered in poppies by school children. The red petals ensuring that the Somme stands for bloodshed and death, not life and victory.

The focus on death and 'sacrifice' is nowhere more epitomised than at the Thiepval Memorial to the Missing. The tiny village of Thiepval in the heart of the Somme battlefield was fortified by the Germans and became a

Lochnagar Crater, La Boisselle, France. Every year on 1st July a dawn service takes place with thousands of poppy petals being let into the crater. (*Robert Perry*)

major objective on the opening day of the battle. That it was not captured until the end of September is testament to the efforts it took to capture it at all. Designed by Sir Edwin Lutyens, a giant memorial now towers over the wrecked former village. On it are inscribed the names of 72,195 British and Commonwealth soldiers who died on the Somme and have no known grave. The architectural historian Vincent Scully called it 'a silent scream',[5] a protest against the unimaginable suffering of the battle. The historian Jay Winter referred to it as 'an extraordinary statement in abstract language about mass death and the impossibility of triumphalism.'[6] It is difficult not to be impressed by its imposing character, yet it exudes no hint of victory, only mass loss of life, which in some ways

Thiepval Memorial to the Missing. *(Ryan Gearing)*

diminishes the achievement of those it remembers.

In Flanders the situation is similar. The Ypres Salient was just as bloody as the Somme and overwhelmingly 'British'. As with the Somme, the entire area is smothered with cemeteries, monuments and memorials. Sections of trenches have been preserved or recreated, museums show glimpses of the underground war, and most dramatic of all, on Ypres' eastern walls, can be found the Menin Gate. Designed by Sir Reginald Blomfield and unveiled in 1927, the memorial sits astride the exit from Vauban's fortifications taken by so many British and Commonwealth soldiers to the surrounding battlefields, many of whom now have their names engraved on its stone walls. Altogether 54,440 names adorn the structure, all of which relate to those dead who have no known grave, men who now form the ranks of the missing. As moving and poignant as the memorial is, those killed with no known grave after 16th August 1917 are not represented. These soldiers are remembered at the nearby Tyne Cot Cemetery. Considering the Third Battle of Ypres, also known as Passchendaele (31st July–10th November 1917), was one of the bloodiest battles fought in the Salient, the absence of its missing on the Menin Gate makes the cost of the fighting in Flanders even more mind-boggling.

Again, the remembrance poppy plays its part in the Salient, as it does in Picardy. Many of the plastic and paper flowers are pressed into the joins of the monument's name

bearing plaques, and at the nightly remembrance service wreaths are left by various organisations and schoolchildren who visit to pay their respects. For Remembrance Day 2011, a field of cardboard poppies was planted next to the memorial, mimicking the better-known buttonhole version. The In Flanders Fields Museum, one of the most highly regarded institutions dedicated to the war, has its home in Ypres' once immolated medieval Cloth Hall. Its logo is a poppy with barbed wire for a stem. The town itself is fully geared up for tourism and the museum shop contains the same plethora of poppy related goods that can be found across the Somme. Nevertheless, it is the Menin Gate that dominates the town and although it wasn't always the case, thousands pack under its arches nightly to hear the Last Post played, many wearing the poppy. Again, the focus is on

School children from South Bromsgrove High in Worcestershire participate in the Last Post ceremony at the Menin Gate. (*South Bromsgrove High School*)

the dead, not the living, and arguably not the missing, so overpowering is the emotional response to the memorial.

Just outside Ypres is Essex Farm Cemetery, site of McCrae's epiphany, and the grave of one of the youngest soldiers to die on the Western Front – Valentine Joe Strudwick, just 15 years old when killed on 14th January 1916. The cemetery contains 1,200 graves. Yet, daily tour buses pull up on the grass verge and their occupants walk through the rows of headstones until they reach Strudwick's resting place. So well used is this processional route that the grass has to be regularly replaced. There the visitors pause, lay poppy wreaths and singular flowers, and then return the way they came, back to the buses and on to the next site. Here, the poppy seemingly stands for an individual, not for the other 1,199 who share the same space, or even for McCrae, or for that matter Lieutenant Alexis Helmer. That is not to say that the death of Strudwick is not worthy of attention or remembrance, the fact that the conflict consumed so many young is one of its saddest legacies,

At the rear of Essex Farm Cemetery, are battlefield remains in the form of a British concrete bunker. It was renovated and preserved in the 1990s as the site of a British Army Advanced Dressing Station.
(Ryan Gearing)

Two of the moving statues at Vladslo Cemetery. (*Simon Gregor*)

but war is often the deathbed of youth. The abundance of poppies around that particular grave provides a metaphor for the symmetry of remembrance across the front.

Siegfried Sassoon referred to the Menin Gate as a 'Sepulchre of Crime', imagining it somehow glorified the dead and missing. Although Sassoon may have been in the minority with his view, certainly the memorial has become a political symbol. Politicians of all denominations regularly visit the site, keen to be photographed, poppy firmly secured in the lapel, beneath the iconic structure. National sports teams visit, as do celebrities and others in the public eye. School trips arrive daily and bands often play at the nightly ceremony ensuring the memorial's capacity to move remains undiminished.

The raw power of the Menin Gate is hard for Ypres to shake. It draws in a great number of people, which in turn support the area's commercial infrastructure, yet Ypres does not wish to be forever associated with death and destruction. Today, Ypres portrays itself as a place of peace, and for somewhere that has known such devastation it is perhaps well qualified to do so. But for it to truly be a centre of peace it must come to terms with the memory of all who died in the Salient, not just the victors. The German dead and missing have no such grand memorials – after all, the invaders lost. There are four cemeteries in the area that cater for the German war dead; Hooglede, Langemarck, Menen and Vladslo – and none contain dominating memorials visited daily by thousands. There is not even an official figure for the German dead in Flanders, but the mass graves in these four locations account for a great number of them. The estimations are that there are around 83,000 German soldiers still missing – more than the number of British and Commonwealth names that appear on the Menin Gate. Instead of bright memorials, Langemarck and Vladslo contain moving statues, far more sombre in nature than anything found in British cemeteries. At Langemarck Emil Krieger's statue of four larger-than-life figures overlooks the mass graves, and at Vladslo, Käthe

Kollwitz's sculpture mourns the loss of her son. Both places are amongst the most sombre in the Salient.

At German cemeteries right across the front there are no remembrance flowers, save an occasional poppy left by a British visitor, but remembrance flora is also in the main absent from French cemeteries. The two main ossuaries at Notre Dame de Lorrette and Douaumont represent the death toll in a very different manner to their British counterparts. Situated on the heights of the Lorette spur, Notre Dame is the largest French military cemetery in the world. Its crosses surround the main ossuary, and the remains of some twenty thousand *poilu* lie in mass graves. The result of this approach is that the war's dead are instead represented on memorials in almost every French

The Douaumont ossuary and cemetery. The ten month Battle of Verdun claimed over 700,000 casualties..
(*Simon Gregor*)

village, town and city, but the remains themselves are concentrated in two main areas. The effect is particularly evident at Verdun, a place seemingly unable to move on from the conflict, forever destined to remind the world of the price France paid to free itself from the grip of the war. At Douaumont, the remains of some 130,000 are preserved in the giant ossuary, visible through windows along the base of the structure, graphically representing the cost of war in more visceral detail than headstones alone are capable of. Even the ossuary communicates the pain the nation felt, taking on the appearance of a huge sword, thrust deep into the soil of France right up to its hilt. The image is so poignant that blue cornflowers are not required to make visitors cogitate on the terrible price played in blood and misery.

In Britain, the Western Front, or at least its memory, is transported closer to home. Almost every urban space in the country somewhere contains a war memorial or role of honour, bedecked in poppies the year round, but more so during November each year. The cenotaph in Whitehall takes centre stage during remembrance ceremonies on Armistice Day, acting as a focus of grief for the dead of all conflicts since 1914. Like the poppy, it is also a contested object, as images of a student swinging from its flags during a 2010 demonstration testify to. Whether in France, Belgium, Canada, London or the quiet villages of England, the Western Front is seen as a place to be revered, not celebrated. A place where the dead are valued above the living and where the contemporary realities of the war are ignored in favour of modern day impressions of a 100-year-old conflict. The remembrance poppy enables this reality, unknowingly wielded as a tool of propaganda, used to push one perspective over another.

Repatriating men home either during or after the conflict was simply not practical, so officers and enlisted men share the same cemeteries right across the Western Front. They lie amongst farmland and urban sprawl, their memory burning brightly for all to see. Yet because the battlefields have been reclaimed, those who died are seen out of context with the landscapes in which they perished.

The grave of Private Jack Banks rests beside five of his fallen comrades from the Durham Light Infantry in the Normandy campaign. Like that of Strudwick's in Essex Farm Cemetery in Flanders, 16-year-old Jack's headstone is always the focus of poppies. (*Ryan Gearing*)

The Cenotaph in London is pictured surrounded by wreaths of poppies. At its unveiling in 1919 the base of the original monument was spontaneously covered in wreaths to the dead and missing from The Great War. Such was the extent of public enthusiasm for the construction it was decided that The Cenotaph should become a permanent and lasting memorial. Built in Portland stone, it was unveiled in 1920. The inscription reads simply 'The Glorious Dead'. (© Crown copyright 2010)

The march of modernity may make this inevitable, but the result is that the myths of how and, more importantly, where they died are reinforced. The battle-zones of 1914–1918 were the product of social, military, industrial and technological ideology – ideology far removed from the modern day equivalent. In the century that has past since the beginning of the war this new memorial landscape has led many to think of the First World War as being distinct in terms of death toll or the brutality of modern warfare, yet the Second World War was every bit as bloody, violent and miserable as its predecessor. In the hundred years between Waterloo and the Battle of Loos seismic changes in the approach to those who perished in war occurred. After Waterloo the bones of the dead were ground up for fertiliser and many of their teeth were used in dentistry – something unthinkable to early twentieth century society. The notoriety of the remembrance poppy and its links to new battle-zones, the power of modern warfare and the massive casualty figures it caused, undoubtedly helped to change these attitudes after 1918. Despite the sacred character of the Western Front, visitors to the area will also notice the roadside memorials to those who died during the Franco Prussian war, fought only a generation before 1914. These now appear dishevelled, and are in stark contrast to those of the Great War, but as time passes and the centenary fades it is impossible not to wonder if the First World War's memorial objects will not go the same way. Since the 1920s the conflict has been remembered in relation to the new landscape strata systematically draped across the old front lines, but in the twenty-first century, it increasingly appears that the future of the war's memory will be in the hands of the modern media.

References

1. Jünger, E. (2004). *Storm of Steel.* London: Penguin Classics. P 98.
2. Sassoon, S. (1997). *Memoirs of an Infantry Officer.* London: Faber and Faber. P 148.
3. Dyer, G. (2009). *The Missing of the Somme.* Phoenix: London. P 12.
4. Gough, P. (2004). 'Sites in the Imagination: The Beaumont Hamel Newfoundland Memorial on the Somme.' *Cultural Geographies* Ch11: Pp 235–258.
5. Winter, J. (2009). *Sites of Memory, Sites of Mourning: The Great War in European Cultural History.* New York: Cambridge University Press. P 105.
6. *Ibid:* P 107.

The Future of the Past

The remembrance poppy is as much a contested object as the Western Front's palimpsest landscape and the loss of life it grew to represent. To some, the flower is the defining symbol of sacrifice during the First World War, to others a totem to the human cost of all wars, and to others still a travesty employed to justify state-sponsored killing on an industrial scale – a true 'sepulchre of crime'. Despite its multi-function, it has undoubtedly facilitated the continued and very public memory of the First World War, but in the twenty-first century media-dominated world, television, social networks and the printed press are destined to play a major role in its future impact, For these are the new wielders of poppy propaganda.

The appearance of the remembrance poppy on television appears to many to arrive earlier and earlier each year. In 2010, the BBC began requiring all who appeared on camera to wear a poppy two weeks before Armistice Day, and the Corporation is no stranger to the politicking behind the flower. In 2001, presenters on foreign arms of the BBC were banned from wearing the poppy so as not offend those who are not British.[1] Conversely, in Britain, being seen to wear the poppy was deemed so important that the newsreader, Hew Edwards, once had to have one fitted to

POPPYGANDA

his jacket halfway through the news, and in 2003 Jonathan Ross allegedly had a poppy digitally superimposed onto him so as not to cause offence.[2] It is probably unfair to single out the BBC in this regard and the majority of network channels in the UK face the same dilemmas. As long as it is perceived that viewers are passionately for the remembrance poppy, the story will be the same every year. Yet, in a country with a dynamic population, who can say if this attitude will persist or not, particularly after 2018?

The perceived influence of the public looms large in the media's decisions. In 2014, the singer Joss Stone collaborated with the Royal British Legion to release the Official Poppy Appeal Song. The BBC, perhaps rather counter intuitively, refused to place the song on its official playlists (although it did receive some airtime on BBC Radio 2) stating that the

Joss Stone featuring Jeff Beck performs 'No Man's Land' (Poppy Appeal Single 2014) by Rupert Bryan. (*deweysworld.com*)

BBC's producers knew the music taste of its listeners. The decision was reported in less than flattering terms in all the major UK newspapers. The *Channel 4 News* presenter, John Snow, caused a great deal of controversy in 2006 by refusing to wear a poppy on air, accusing those who criticised him of 'poppy fascism'. The remembrance poppy has become so politicised that Snow had a valid point, yet his decision not to wear one only added to the body of poppy politics, fuelling the fire even further.

As the media has become more intrusive and influential in daily life, the relationship between the remembrance poppy and celebrity has both deepened and darkened. Television programmes such as *Strictly Come Dancing* and *The X Factor* have been at the forefront of the 'bling poppy', taking a symbol of remembrance and changing it into a fashion statement. Although these two shows are not the only ones, together they account for many millions of

Katherine Jenkins performing on BBC's *Strictly Come Dancing*. (BBC)

viewers, both series run over the course of November each year, and the approach to poppy wearing undoubtedly influences many. Type 'bling poppy' into Amazon.co.uk and almost 1,400 results are returned. The Royal British Legion receives little or no money from these fashion poppies, and increasingly they are becoming so stylised that they barely resemble the flower at all. Nevertheless, in a world of instant social media, celebrity endorsement can do wonders for any product. The Legion may not receive money from fashion poppies, but a celebrity wearing one is likely to increase sales of the more traditional version, or simply raise awareness of the cause. In 2014, celebrities worked with Transport For London to raise money for the Royal British Legion's appeal voicing announcements on the London tube and

Susan Boyle was joined by 80 members of two of Scotland's Military Wives Choirs to launch the 2012 Scottish Poppy Appeal.
(*Scottish Poppy Appeal*)

bus networks. The footballers; John Terry, Joey Barton and Andros Townsend, all recorded announcements for stations near their respective club grounds, and Sir Terry Wogan, Joanna Lumley and Brian Blessed, among others, also contributed. The only non-English people to publicly take part were, Arséne Wenger, the Arsenal Football Club manager, and Mikel Arteta, the Arsenal captain. Wenger is a Frenchman and Arteta a Spaniard. Wenger's reasons for contributing were that he respected the country he lives and works in. It is difficult not to wonder what the response might have been should he have chosen to wear a blue cornflower instead of a poppy.

Over Armistice Day sportsmen and women wearing poppies on their kit has become commonplace. In 2011, FIFA refused the England football team permission to wear the flower on their shirts during a friendly game against Spain, which resulted in the inevitable outcry. Domestically, the poppy is embroidered onto most professional sports kits around 11th November each year, but even this causes problems. The need to be seen to comply with this homogenisation has itself become politicised. In England, the Football League contains many foreign players and managers. What German, Argentinean, Turkish and Austrian players and managers (to name but a few) think of wearing the poppy on their chests, or what their fellow countrymen think of it at home, is difficult to know, but it would take a brave footballer to refuse to wear the poppy. It is perhaps not surprising then, that it is a rare occurrence, although this is exactly what

London Mayor Boris Johnson launched London's Poppy Day appeal in 2014, raising the roof of a poppy-adorned Liverpool Street station with actor Brian Blessed who completed his national service as a parachutist in the RAF. *(Rupert Frere / © Crown copyright 2014)*

James McClean of Wigan Athletic did in 2014:

For me to wear a poppy would be as much a gesture of disrespect for the innocent people who lost their lives in the Troubles – and Bloody Sunday especially. . . It would be seen as an act of disrespect to my people.[4]

McClean was perfectly within his rights not to wear the poppy, and to many in Ireland the poppy remains an intensely politicised object, the material realties of which can be seen at many places on the Western Front, not least in the contrasting memorials at the Ulster Tower on the Somme or at Thiepval every Armistice Day. The remembrance poppy has been adopted by other sports too, not least by professional cycling. In 2014, the route

Arsenal observe a minutes silence for remembrance day – Barclays Premier League – Arsenal v West Bromwich Albion – Emirates Stadium 5 November 2011. (© *EMPICS* / *TopFoto*)

POPPYGANDA

The 2014 Tour de France inspired a 'King of the Mountains' style cycling shirt which sprang up throughout Ypres' shops. (*Author*)

of the Tour de France took the peloton along sections of the old Western Front and riders for the Omega Pharma Quickstep team wore a poppy on their shirts when the fifth stage left from the main square in Ypres. In 2015, the Tour traversed further sections of the front, and the route over the next few years will almost certainly follow suit.

The corruption of the remembrance poppy in the media, television and sport undoubtedly has its political ramifications, but however influential these are, when the

Jonathan Yeo,
Tony Blair,
2007.
Oil on canvas.
75cm x 75cm

same process takes place directly within the political arena, the consequences can be far more severe. The sight of politicians bedecked in poppies is not unusual, but the irony of those same politicians wearing poppies while the country is at war can be a bitter pill to swallow. Tony Blair's first official portrait was unveiled in 2008, and it featured the former prime minister wearing a poppy on his lapel. During the Blair premiership, Britain went to war on four

POPPYGANDA

These hand embroidered poppy towels were made in Afghanistan amongst the legacies of twenty-first century conflict. Afghanistan is a country known for its opium poppy production, some of which becomes heroin and is sold in Britain and the US. Much of the rest is used for morphine. The soothing fruit of the poppy provides relief for injured soldiers, some of whom die and are memorialised by the remembrance version of the flower, demonstrating the complexity of the poppy's biography. (*Mothers for Peace*)

occasions; Kosovo, Sierra Leone, Afghanistan and most notably in Iraq. Academic research in the United States, Canada and Iraq[5] estimates that almost half a million people have lost their lives since the 2003 invasion of Iraq. In 2010, the Muslim extremist, Emdamur Choudhury, burned remembrance poppies while chanting anti-war slogans. He was promptly charged and appeared before the courts. Found guilty of abusive behaviour and, rather sensibly, given the minimum possible sentence, the judge argued that his behaviour was 'a calculated and deliberate insult to the dead and those who mourn them'. But he also made clear that Choudhury had the right to voice his opinions in what, after all, is a free country.

Whether Blair or Choudhury's conduct towards the poppy is perceived as acceptable or not largely depends on an ideological perspective, but the inescapable fact is that in both cases the poppy was used as a propaganda tool (or weapon). Things become even more confused when the links between the remembrance poppy, the opium

Sepoy Khudadad
Khan VC, 129th
Battalion, Duke
of Connaught's
Own Baluchi
Regiment, the
first Indian and
Muslim to win
the Victoria
Cross. After
the war Khan
returned to India,
and continued
to serve in the
Indian Army. In
1971 he died at
home in Pakistan,
aged 84.

poppy, morphine, warfare and Afghanistan's production of heroin are added to the mix.[6] Afghanistan currently grows more raw opium for heroin production than ever before, despite a decade long war fought by the West. The irony is compounded by the knowledge that most of this crop is exported to the United States and Britain.

In 2010, Prime Minister David Cameron led a coalition trade delegation to China, and he, along with George Osborne, Vince Cable and Michal Gove were all pictured toasting an agreement while wearing the remembrance poppy. China, Britain and the poppy, at least with regard to its opium strain, have a long and tortured history and the Chinese authorities had asked the British not to wear the flower in deference to the way it was viewed as a symbol of their oppression by European powers during the nineteenth century. The British refused, with one delegate stating, 'We informed them that they (the poppies) meant a great deal to us and we would be wearing them all the same.'[7]

The twenty-first century's wars in the Middle East involving Britain have again elevated the remembrance poppy in the public's conscience and the way it is politically deployed has, as a

SEPOY KHUDADAD KHAN, V.C., 129TH BALUCHIS.

consequence, been further brought to the fore. In 2014, the Islamic Society of Britain produced a hijab featuring the flower, with the proceeds from its sale going to the Royal British Legion's Poppy Appeal. The hijab was designed to commemorate Khudadad Khan who was the first Muslim to win the Victoria Cross. Sepoy Khan was awarded his medal for actions at Hollebeke in 1914[8] and the hijab was meant to foster community in the United Kingdom and remember that many thousands of Muslims fought for the Allied cause during the conflict. Public opinion was mixed. Some accused the Islamic Society of Britain of trying to appropriate the symbol for their own ends, others suggested that the hijab was a religious garment and that political statements had no place on it. To others still, it was seen as a way that Muslim women could pay their respects.

Poppy Hijab. Designed by Tabinda-Kauser Ishaq, a London College of Fashion student, to appeal to British Muslims wishing to mark Remembrance Day. (*Artefact Magazine*)

Again, ideology determined the response and it is doubtful that the hijab did much to change entrenched views on the poppy one way or the other – Sepoy Khan's extraordinary bravery appeared to be lost in the political discourse.

Groups on the far right have long been accused of appropriating British symbols for their own end. By the early 1990s the Union Jack (or the Union Flag, if you prefer) had become so associated with the National Front and British National Party that many had begun to turn their back on it. It took the rise of 'Cool Britannia' (and perhaps a Spice Girl's dress?) to bring it back into the mainstream. The poppy has also survived repeated attempts to appropriate it for 'nationalistic' purposes. The far right group, Britain First, used the poppy in an attempt to gain support and notoriety by attaching an image of it to their social media posts and asking people to forward the image on, or press 'Like' to show their support. Unwittingly, perhaps, these posts have been forwarded many hundreds of thousands of times. The Royal British Legion was forced to threaten Britain First with legal action, arguing that the remembrance poppy was their trademark and not to be used as a political symbol.

Nevertheless, the remembrance poppy is a political symbol, wielded by the prime minister abroad and those with their own political agenda at home. Despite the Legion's best efforts, the 'Britishness' of the poppy had been seized upon, and the Legion must take some of the responsibility for

POPPYGANDA

this. In 2013, a representative of UKIP laid a poppy wreath at a war memorial in Plymouth causing consternation and outcry from other political parties. The wreath was a typical example, with the UKIP badge at the centre. UKIP countered that they had laid the same wreaths the year before and no one had taken any notice. They argued that because 2013 was an election year, other parties were using it to try and associate UKIP with the far right. Despite the disapproval, a certain amount of hypocrisy was evident. The wreath had been ordered directly from the Royal British Legion and the Legion themselves commented that wreaths were made for all the main political parties every year. If the poppy is not to be politicised, it must be asked why the Royal British Legion are culpable of doing so?

The art installation 'Blood Swept Lands and Seas of Red' at the Tower of London. (© *Crown copyright 2014*)

UKIP and the poppy have found media attention more recently when their leader, Nigel Farage, was pictured weeping before the Tower of London's memorial display. *Blood Swept Lands and Seas of Red* was the title of a moving piece of art installed at the Tower for Remembrance Day in 2014. A staggering 888,246 ceramic poppies, one for every British and Commonwealth soldier that died in the First World War, were 'planted' into the grass of the Tower's moat. Millions visited the exhibit, including the author of this book, and it was indeed a moving and fitting tribute. The ceramic flowers were later sold, raising an estimated £11m for British charities such as Help the Heroes and the Royal British Legion. Even though the public response to the display was overwhelmingly positive, because it involved the poppy, it was not without its controversy. *The Guardian* newspaper's art critic, Jonathan Jones, branded the display a 'deeply aestheticised, petrified and toothless war memorial', going on to describe it as being 'fake, trite and inward-looking – a UKIP-style memorial'.[10] The response was predictable with many in the press and on social media calling for Jones' head. It could of course be argued that Farage's tears cemented Jones' point. But in fairness to the politician, many who visited the memorial were deeply moved and if the remembrance poppy had not become such a political weapon Farage's tears wouldn't have been viewed differently to anyone else's. Even grief,

POPPYGANDA

genuine or otherwise, in front of the remembrance flower now has to be legitimised.

In May 2015 the relationship between the remembrance poppy and loss was brought into sharp focus by the tragic death of Olive Cook. Olive, aged 92, had been selling poppies for the Royal British Legion for 76 years. So well known was her charity work, that when she was found dead at the bottom of Bristol's Avon Gorge, reports in the media suggested she had been driven to suicide to escape the relentless attention of charities requesting donations from her. Even though her family stated that the intrusion of other charities was not that serious, this didn't stop the media suggesting so. The idea of this symbol of remembrance causing death was too good a story to resist

The tragic death of 92-year-old Olive Cook, brought the remembrance poppy into sharp focus. After selling poppies for the Royal British Legion for 76 years, her body was found at the bottom of Bristol's Avon Gorge. (*Third Sector Magazine*)

– it sold papers, increased viewing figures and swelled website hits.

As chapters are added to the remembrance poppy's biography, the role of the media in the public perception of the poppy is set to increase, but modern ideas of 'media' are also changing. Social media is now as important as the print and broadcast media in influencing opinions and reaching the public. In 2014 it is estimated that Remembrance Day generated over 560 million impressions on Twitter alone.[11] Facebook avatars across the world are changed to picture the flower, and individuals in the public eye are shamed instantly if spotted without the poppy on their lapels. Social media gives individuals a power of speech that was previously held only by commercial media organisations, meaning that before long the conglomerates that have dictated poppy etiquette for years will likely become subservient to the public. Will this mean the poppy begins to fade, or will it be catapulted into newfound popularity?

The truth is that no mater how much intellectual freedom social media gives individuals, it simultaneously ties them into the way that news is now reported. Instant updates on Twitter or from media outlets appear regularly on mobile devices, and are then instantly forwarded to social media sites by those that deem them worthy of attention. Yet the way that twenty-first century warfare is now conducted, and the way it is portrayed by the modern

media, can have serious repercussions in terms of the way the public understand it.

The ongoing conflicts in the Middle East, often focused on the continuing crisis between Palestine and Israel, the march of IS in Syria and Iraq (and beyond), and an increasing sectarian divide within and between faiths in many countries are all types of conflict seemingly far removed from the Western Front a century ago. Intense coverage of these conflagrations often distances us in Britain from events rather than bringing us closer to them. The crisis in Ukraine highlights how modern warfare affects the way that people experience, or feel, conflict. Many soldiers in Ukraine wear no insignia, and it's often unclear which side they represent. This makes them 'invisible', despite daily battles in the streets

The number 30 double decker bus in Tavistock Square, which was destroyed by a terrorist bomb in July 2007.
(© *PA Photos / Topfoto*)

and nightly television footage of these phantom soldiers. So great is the reach of modern conflict that the passengers of flight MH17 became devastating victims of this war, and their apparent distance from the battlefield, reinforced by impressions in the media of the conflict being isolated and far away, made little difference to the mechanical weaponry employed on the ground. The idea of wearing poppies for those passengers is perhaps as relevant as wearing them for the soldiers who perished in the mud of the Western Front, yet the media is yet to make the connection.

Twenty-first century conflict has increased the idea of battle-zones exponentially from their birth during the First World War. The 2001 World Trade Centre attacks in New York, the 2004 train bombings in Madrid, the 2005 atrocities on London public transport, and the 2015 shootings at the Charlie Hebdo offices in Paris all show that in modern warfare battle-zones are no longer precisely definable or identifiable – as likely to exist in a Middle Eastern desert as on a bus in a European city. In turn this makes them far more accessible to the public, but where does the poppy fit into this new type of conflict? How, if at all, will the media's apparatus, or individuals wielding its modern incarnation in the form of social media, move the poppy's biography forward? Perhaps it will take another World War, or a series of grand and hugely costly battles. The reality is that the World Wars of the twentieth century are unlikely to be repeated in the near future, and more likely the next reincarnation of the poppy as an object of remembrance will be an iconic photograph of it growing by a victim of domestic terrorism. No matter how the media or politicians want to portray today's warfare, it has changed a great deal since 1918. But it is still a bloody business, and those consumed by its furore deserve to be remembered, even if it is only in the blood-red reflection of a small paper flower.

References

1. http://www.telegraph.co.uk/news/uknews/1361358/BBC-defends-ban-on-TV-presenters-wearing-poppies.html
2. http://www.theguardian.com/media/mediamonkeyblog/2013/oct/16/bbc-poppy-row
3. http://www.telegraph.co.uk/culture/tvandradio/bbc/11220140/Poppy-appeal-single-rejected-from-BBC-playlist.html
4. http://www.irishtimes.com/news/politics/standing-up-against-the-poppy-and-the-perversion-of-sport-1.1998282
5. http://www.bbc.co.uk/news/world-middle-east-24547256
6. Saunders, N. J. (2013). The Poppy: A Cultural History from Ancient Egypt to Flanders Fields and Afghanistan. London: Oneworld.
7. http://www.theguardian.com/politics/blog/2010/nov/10/david-cameron-poppy-china-michael-white
8. https://livesofthefirstworldwar.org/lifestory/2247379
9. http://www.independent.co.uk/news/uk/politics/ukip-poppy-wreath-sparks-row-over-remembrance-day-party-politics-8936626.html
10. http://www.huffingtonpost.co.uk/2014/11/01/guardian-poppies-jonathan-jones-_n_6086802.html
11. http://www.coosto.com/en/resources/blog/remembrance-during-poppy-day-hot-topic-on-social-media

Epilogue

Although the poppy has a long and colourful history dating back many centuries before the First World War, in the public psyche it will always be associated with that conflict. The story of the Great War has been rewritten many times, and historians still argue today over the rights and wrongs of fighting the conflict, the complexity (or not) of the tactics employed, the efficacy of the weaponry, the questionable outcome and the predictability of what followed some twenty years later. The poppy has experienced a similar journey and a century after McCrae penned his poem, this flower of remembrance has travelled a great distance from that private moment in the trenches outside Ypres. Today there is no one left alive anywhere in the world that experienced combat during the First World War on the Western Front. The realities of that conflict are hidden in the material culture it left behind – a complex and ambiguous mix of artefacts, memory and myth. As this book has explored, the First World War soldier had a unique relationship with the landscapes in which he fought. As he witnessed the devastating effect that human technological and industrial prowess could have on nature and mankind, the boundaries between people and landscape, objects and meaning, and life and death became at times indistinguishable. To McCrae, the poppy was a symbol of that complex relationship, a natural object that could thrive amongst so much destruction, reflecting the existential experience of the front. It was so prevalent in the war's battle-zones that McCrae's poem struck a chord with many after it was published in December 1915. Yet the depth of feeling the flower and those who saw it grow amongst the carnage of the front shared can only be guessed at today.

The Royal British Legion states that the remembrance poppy is a symbol of peace, yet the assertion that McCrae intended it to be so is debateable. The final verse of *In Flanders Fields* seems to hint otherwise:

> *Take up our quarrel with the foe:*
> *To you from failing hands we throw*
> *The torch; be yours to hold it high.*
> *If ye break faith with us who die*
> *We shall not sleep, though poppies grow*
> *In Flanders fields.*

What McCrae meant by those words is open to interpretation, and further highlights the complexity of the human engagement with modern war. That he felt anger at so much loss is understandable, as is the notion that unless Germany was beaten the deaths of many would be in vain. Does McCrae's poem stand for peace and an end to war, or the prosecution of those that obstruct or seek to destroy the values he held dear? The answer is that it is impossible to project the thoughts of a single man surrounded by the full trauma of the war onto life, politics and warfare almost a century later. Of course, this doesn't stop many trying.

No matter what McCrae really meant by his final verse, its ambiguity is perhaps the answer to what the remembrance poppy should represent. That Moina Michaels saw the flower in the same way as McCrae is highly unlikely. However personal it may have appeared to her, it was almost certainly more so to McCrae, who witnessed the visceral realities of this new warfare at close quarters – while Michaels was far removed. In 2015, the poppy is set to loom even larger in the public conscious and the next few years will likely bear witness to yet more controversy surrounding it. The flower was reborn in the battle-zones of the Great War, recycled, given new purpose and meaning. It shared the same space as destroyed humanity and annihilated nature, and as it bloomed amongst the carnage and destruction, it offered hope that the once the guns had ceased firing life would flourish once again, and a new world would be created from the destruction of the war.

No matter how the poppy is represented, from the moment McCrae penned his poem, and particularly its last verse, the flower has been a tool of propaganda, whether to call for an end to war or its continuation to defend

shared values. It is no surprise that this has happened –
it is all just another stage in the flower's enduring story
as a piece of Great War material culture. What is certain
is that around 11th November this year millions will
pin one to their lapels and millions of others will not.
Too often the remembrance poppy is used to justify the
human experience and perceived futility of a conflict
that a hundred years later the public cannot hope to fully
understand. Many groups vociferously claim ownership,
but if the history of the poppy has told us anything, it is
that it belongs to no one and flourishes in the remains
of cultures that thought they understood its power. That
the flower has now become a tool of propaganda should
not be in doubt, but its public prominence and intensely
contested nature ensures that echoes of those who fell in
the Great War, and all wars since, will annually be brought
to the fore, thereby ensuring that we will remember them.

Bibliography

Blunden, E. (2009). *Undertones of War*. London: Penguin Classics.

Carpenter, H. (1977). *J.R.R Tolkien: A Biography*. London: George Allen & Unwin Ltd.

--- (ed). (1995). *The Letters of J.R.R Tolkien*. London: Houghton Mifflin.

Das, S. (2008). *Touch and Intimacy in First World War Literature*. Cambridge: Cambridge University Press.

Dyer, G. (2009). *The Missing of the Somme*. London: Phoenix.

Gough, P. (2004). Sites in the Imagination: The Beaumont Hamel Newfoundland Memorial on the Somme. *Cultural Geographies* 11: 235 – 258.

Jünger, E. (2004). *Storm of Steel*. London: Penguin Classics.

Masefield, J. (2003). *The Old Frontline*. Barnsley: Pen and Sword Military Classics.

Mosse, G. (1990). *Fallen Soldiers: Reshaping the Memory of the World Wars*. New York: Oxford University Press

Remarque, E. (1929). *All Quiet on the Western Front*. Boston: Little Brown.

Sassoon, S. (1997). *Memoirs of an Infantry Officer*. London: Faber and Faber.

Saunders, N, J. (2004). Material Culture and Conflict. The Great War, 1914-2003. In N.J. Saunders. (ed.). *Matters of Conflict. Material culture, memory and the First World War*. Abingdon: Routledge.

--- (2013). *The Poppy. A Cultural History from Ancient Egypt to Flanders Fields and Afghanistan*. London: Oneworld.

Smith, L. (2009). *Drawing Fire*. London: Collins.

Tolkien, J, R, R. (2008). *The Two Towers (The Second Book of The Lord of The Rings)*. London: Harper Collins.

Winter, J. (2009). *Sites of Memory, Sites of Mourning: The Great War in European Cultural History*. New York: Cambridge University Press

Websites

www.telegraph.co.uk

www.theguardian.com

www.bbc.co.uk

www.irishtimes.com

www.livesofthefirstworldwar.org

www.independent.co.uk

www.huffingtonpost.co.uk

www.durandgroup.org.uk

www.iwm.org.uk

www.inflandersfields.be

www.historial.org

www.modernconflictarchaeology.com